DATE DUE

5·31·13			

TITLES IN THE SERIES

CAREER CHOICES FOR STUDENTS OF:

**ART
BUSINESS
COMMUNICATIONS AND JOURNALISM
COMPUTER SCIENCE
ECONOMICS
ENGLISH
HISTORY
MATHEMATICS
POLITICAL SCIENCE AND GOVERNMENT
PSYCHOLOGY**

CAREER CHOICES FOR UNDERGRADUATES
CONSIDERING:

**LAW
AN M.B.A.**

CAREER CHOICES FOR THE

FOR THE

90's

FOR STUDENTS OF

ART

WALKER AND COMPANY
NEW YORK

First published in the United States of America in 1990
by Walker Publishing Company, Inc.

Published simultaneously in Canada by Thomas Allen & Son
Canada, Limited, Markham, Ontario

Library of Congress Cataloging-in-Publication Data
Career choices for students of art / by Career Associates.
Includes bibliographical references.
ISBN 0-8027-7324-9
1. Art—Vocational guidance—United States. I. Career
Associates.
N6505.C34   1990
702.3'73—dc20   89-70519
CIP

Printed in the United States of America

2 4 6 8 10 9 7 5 3

CAREER ASSOCIATES

ACKNOWLEDGMENTS

We gratefully acknowledge the help of the many people who spent time talking to our research staff about employment opportunities in their fields. This book would not have been possible without their assistance. Our thanks, too, to Catalyst, which has one of the best career libraries in the country in its New York, NY, offices, and to the National Society for Internships and Experiential Education, Raleigh, NC, which provided information on internship opportunities for a variety of professions.

The chapter on legal careers came about only through the excellent efforts of Lynn Stephens Strudler, Assistant Dean of the New York University School of Law Placement Office; special thanks, also, to the staff of researchers and interviewers who took time from their duties as law placement officers to gather the information in this chapter. The following individuals and organizations were particularly generous with their time and evaluations of the information contained-in this book:

Marge Dover, National Association of Legal Assistants
Robert Kenyon, American Society of Magazine Editors
William Stolgitis, Society for Technical Communication

CONTENTS

What's in this book for you?

WHAT'S IN THIS BOOK FOR YOU?

With the 1990s in full force and the year 2000—the new millenium!—no longer a distant specter, it's more important than ever to look closely at the changes in different industries. Industries, and consequently, a student's career choices have changed dramatically in the last decade. This book is designed to give you the latest information on a range of different career possibilities.

Recent college graduates, no matter what their major has been, too often discover that there is a dismaying gap between their knowledge and planning and the reality of an actual career. Possibly even more unfortunate is the existence of potentially satisfying careers that graduates do not even know about. Although advice from campus vocational counselors, family, friends, and fellow students can be extremely helpful, there is no substitute for a structured exploration of the various alternatives open to graduates.

The Career Choices Series was created to provide you with the means to conduct such an exploration. It gives you specific, up-to-date information about the entry-level job opportunities in a variety of industries relevant to your degree and highlights opportunities that might otherwise be overlooked. Through its many special features—such as sections on internships, qualifications, and working conditions—the Career Choices Series can help you find out where your interests and abilities lie in order to point your search for an entry-level job in a productive direction. This book cannot find you a job—only you can provide the hard work, persistence, and ingenuity that that requires—but it can save you valuable time and energy. By helping you to narrow the range of your search to careers that are truly suitable for you, this book can help make hunting for a job an exciting adventure rather than a dreary—and sometimes frightening—chore.

The book's easy-to-use format combines general information about each of the industries covered with the hard facts that job-hunters must have. An overall explanation of each industry is followed by authoritative material on the job outlook for entry-level candidates, the competition for the openings that exist, and the new opportunities that may arise from such factors as expansion and technological development. There is a listing of employers by type and by geographic location and a sampling of leading companies by name—by no means all, but enough to give you a good idea of who the employers are.

Many young people are interested in being an entrepreneur and you'll find a section showing examples of people who have succeeded as entrepreneurs in the different industries. There's also a discussion of "intrapreneurship"—how you can be an entrepreneur with a large company.

The section on how to break into the field is not general how-to-get-a-job advice, but rather zeroes in on ways of getting a foot in the door of a particular industry.

You will find the next section, a description of the major functional areas within each industry, especially valuable in making your initial job choice. For example, communications majors aiming for magazine work can evaluate the editorial end, advertising space sales, circulation, or production. Those interested in accounting are shown the differences between management, government, and public accounting. Which of the various areas described offers you the best chance of an entry-level job? What career paths are likely to follow from that position? Will they help you reach your ultimate career goal? The sooner you have a basis to make the decision, the better prepared you can be.

For every industry treated and for the major functional areas within that industry, you'll learn what your duties—both basic and more challenging—are likely to be, what hours you'll work, what your work environment will be, and what range of salary to expect*. What personal and professional qualifications must you have? How can you move up—and to what? This book tells you.

---

*Salary figures given are the latest available as the book goes to press.

You'll learn how it is possible to overcome the apparent contradiction of the truism, "To get experience you have to have experience." The kinds of extracurricular activities and work experience—summer and/or part-time—that can help you get and perform a job in your chosen area are listed. Internships are another way to get over that hurdle, and specific information is included for each industry.

You'll find a list of the books and periodicals you should read to keep up with the latest trends in an industry you are considering, and the names and addresses of professional associations that can be helpful to you—through student chapters, open meetings, and printed information. Finally, interviews with professionals in each field bring you the experiences of people who are actually working in the kinds of jobs you may be aiming for.

Although your entry-level job neither guarantees nor locks you into a lifelong career path, the more you know about what is open to you, the better chance you'll have for a rewarding work future. The information in these pages will not only give you a realistic basis for a good start, it will help you immeasurably in deciding what to explore further on your own. So good reading, good hunting, good luck, and the best of good beginnings.

BOOK PUBLISHING

Work your way up to become a top editor at one of the world's most prestigious publishing houses. Find that diamond in the rough who goes on to become the next great American novelist. Close a multimillion-dollar deal that will bring one of your publisher's novels to the silver screen. Make sure that limo is waiting for your temperamental star author when he gets off the plane—or better yet, have a limo waiting for *you* to whisk you away to that big meeting on the Coast.

Such are the fantasies book lovers may conjure about working for a book publisher. Sometimes, fantasies like these can come true, just as sometimes a writer's first novel makes it to the top of the best-seller list. More often, however, the realities of a career in book publishing are far less glamorous—just as most first novels are ingloriously laid to rest on the remainder table at your local bookstore.

Yet although the gap between fantasy and reality is wide, book publishing continues to attract a great number of aspiring editors, designers, and publicists. And despite the realities—hard work, anonymity, and relatively low wages—those who forge a career in book publishing often find deep satisfaction in their life's work.

Once upon a time, the book publishing business was renowned for its rock-solid stability: G. P. Putnam's Sons, Harper & Row,

Charles Scribner's Sons, and Doubleday & Co., among others, were privately held businesses that remained essentially unchanged for decades. While some publishers have remained true to their small-business roots, more have become part of the fabric of big business. Hardly a month goes by, it seems, without a major announcement of a buy out, merger, or "joint venture" involving major publishers or their parent companies. Within the space of a few months in the late 1980s, for example, Random House acquired one of its competitors, Crown Publishers Inc.; Random House then worked a "trade" with McGraw-Hill Inc., swapping most of its school textbook operation for McGraw-Hill's trade publishing holdings. Meanwhile, McGraw-Hill, which was also busy selling off the bulk of its magazine publishing business, entered into a cooperative sales agreement with one of its major competitors in the textbook business, Macmillan Co., which had recently been purchased in a long and somewhat bitter takeover by British media mogul Robert Maxwell. So much for stability.

At the same time that major publishers are consolidating, a growing number of fledgling book publishers are finding comfortable niches for themselves. Most of these small publishers specialize in specific areas—for example, Greenwood Press in New Haven, CT, publishes scholarly titles relating to American history, while Mercury House in San Francisco focuses on fiction from new writers. Other niche markets include travel books, cookbooks, sports-related titles, and art books.

With all the changes taking place in the book publishing business, however, a few things remain constant. One is that the job market—particularly in editorial positions—is highly competitive. Another is that because of this keen competition, salaries in book companies are low compared with those in other industries and even those in other publishing areas.

A third constant is that if you're looking to start a publishing career, your best bet is to live in the New York or Boston area. Although many small publishers are now headquartered throughout the country, the major companies, the ones with the most job opportunities, still have the bulk of their operations in these publishing centers.

While editorial work is the most obvious part of book publishing, other career paths are also available. Books don't always sell themselves. Most publishers have sales, marketing, promotion, and advertising departments to spread the word about their titles. Production departments are critical components in the publishing process; production staffers design the interior and exterior of a book and see the book through the manufacturing process. Publicists contact reviewers and other media reporters to ensure that a book gets proper press coverage. Subsidiary rights departments license second-serial rights to other media—reprinters, magazines, book clubs, and TV or film producers.

JOB OUTLOOK

JOB OPENINGS WILL GROW: More slowly than average

COMPETITION FOR JOBS: Keen

Expect the most competition in editorial; other functional areas may be more accessible. If you are considering the sales end of publishing, your chances are better in a smaller company. Textbook publishing is often overlooked as a good place to find publishing jobs.

NEW JOB OPPORTUNITIES: The growing number of small publishers across the nation should boost employment opportunities outside the major publishing centers. Sales and marketing operations of large publishers are often a good place to start in the book business.

GEOGRAPHIC JOB INDEX

Most publishing houses are located in and around New York, NY, the undisputed capital of publishing, Los Angeles, CA, Washington, DC, Chicago, IL, and Boston, MA. Small regional publishers are located throughout the country.

WHO THE EMPLOYERS ARE

PUBLISHERS OF TRADE BOOKS (general interest books, fiction, and nonfiction) and PAPERBACK BOOK PUBLISHERS are the most numerous. Trade houses publish original manuscripts in hardcover and softcover. Paperback houses and divisions produce both reprints of hardback originals and, increasingly, original manuscripts.

SPECIALIZED PUBLISHERS of encyclopedias and dictionaries, reference books, programmed learning materials, multimedia materials, textbooks, and scholarly works represent a major portion of the book industry and offer many opportunities for entry-level people.

MAJOR EMPLOYERS

TRADE PUBLISHERS
Doubleday & Company, New York, NY
Harcourt Brace Jovanovich, New York, NY, San Diego, CA, Washington, DC
Holt, Rinehart & Winston, New York, NY, Orlando, FL
Houghton Mifflin Company, Boston, MA, New York, NY
Little, Brown & Company, Boston, MA
Macmillan Publishing Company, New York, NY
G. P. Putnam's Sons, New York, NY
Random House, New York, NY
Simon and Schuster, New York, NY
Time-Life Books, Alexandria, VA

PAPERBACK PUBLISHERS
Avon Books, New York, NY
Ballantine/DelRey/Fawcett Books, New York, NY
Bantam Books, New York, NY
Dell Publishing Company, New York, NY
New American Library, New York, NY
Simon & Schuster Inc., Pocket Books, New York, NY

Viking Penguin Inc., New York, NY
Warner Books, New York, NY

EDUCATIONAL AND PROFESSIONAL PUBLISHERS
Harcourt Brace Jovanovich, San Diego, CA, Orlando, FL
Holt, Rinehart & Winston, New York, NY, Philadelphia, PA,
    Austin, TX
Houghton Mifflin Company, Boston, MA
McGraw-Hill, Inc., New York, NY
W. W. Norton & Company, New York, NY
Prentice-Hall, Englewood Cliffs, NJ
Scott, Foresman, Glenview, IL
John Wiley and Sons, New York, NY

RELIGIOUS PUBLISHERS
Abingdon Press, Nashville, TN
Baker Book House, Grand Rapids, MI
Baptist Publishing House, El Paso, TX
Fleming H. Revell, Old Tappan, NY
Paulist Press, Mahwah, NJ
The Westminster Press, Philadelphia, PA
Zondervan, Grand Rapids, MI

HOW TO BREAK INTO THE FIELD

Publishing houses often route job applicants through the personnel office. But many jobs are secured by going directly to the head of a department or even to one of the top editors. Contacts are important, even for entry-level people.

Attending a summer publishing institute provides opportunities to sharpen your skills and meet people who are established in the trade. Such institutes include the following:

City University of New York
Graduate Center
Education in Publishing Program
33 W42nd Street, Rm. 1206A
New York, NY 10036

Howard University Press
Book Publishing Institute
2900 Van Ness Street, N.W.
Washington, DC 20008

New York University
Summer Publishing Institute
Center for Publishing
48 Cooper Square
New York, NY 10003

Radcliffe College/Harvard University
The Radcliffe Publishing Courses
6 Ash Street
Cambridge, MA 02138

Stanford University
Stanford Publishing Course
Stanford Alumni Association
Stanford, CA 94305

University of Denver
Publishing Institute
Graduate School of Arts and Humanities
English Dept.
2075 South University, #D-114
Denver, CO 80208

Employment agencies specializing in publishing placement are worth a try, as are help-wanted ads in newspapers and trade magazines.

ENTREPRENEURIAL

Start your own publishing company? The idea may be the ultimate fantasy of book lovers. In fact, a growing number of people are doing just that.

According to some estimates, more that 2,000 titles per year are published by new entrepreneurs. An overwhelming majority of these publishers are writers who have set out to put their own work in print.

The idea of self-publishing isn't new. Writers who have found the doors of mainstream publishers closed to them have long used their own resources to get their books in print. In most cases, writers turn publishers only as long as they need to. Once a mainstream publisher offers to print their work, most self-publishers are more than happy to leave their publishing career behind.

The computer technology boom, however, may well give rise to tremendous growth in the number of small, independent publishers who are in business to do more than publish their own work. Already, there are more than 1,000 such publishers in the U.S. By investing a few thousand dollars in an appropriate desk top publishing system, a would-be publisher can instantly have the resources to bring a manuscript up to the stage at which it's ready to go to press.

Of course, printing a book is only half the battle—the easy half, some might say. Getting a book distributed and sold can be the most costly part of book publishing.

Most small publishers don't have the wherewithal to pay for their own sales staffs; many simply sell their books via mail order. Others use independent distributors and sales reps. These independents typically represent dozens of small and, in some cases, large publishers. They generally work on a commission basis. As the number of small publishers continues to grow, demand for the services of independent distributors and sellers should also rise. This will afford ambitious self-starters another business opportunity.

Computer technology also offers budding intrapreneurs an opportunity to make their marks within book companies. Unlike newspaper and magazine publishers, book publishers for the most part have not computerized their book production operations. The opportunity for significant cost savings is incredible. In some companies that are automated, manuscript preparation costs have fallen by more than 50 percent. Savings like that should be enough to capture the attention of any publisher, and bring suitable rewards to the go-getter in the company who makes the system work.

EDITORIAL

Two functions are involved: acquiring and line editing. Acquisition editors secure publication rights for their houses, and this can be done in a variety of ways. Promising book ideas or good manuscripts may come from authors directly or through their agents. Often an editor will come up with a saleable concept and choose experts or authors to do the writing. Acquiring also involves negotiating advances and arranging author contracts.

Line editing involves working closely with the author to make sure that the manuscript is thorough, well-organized, clear, and well-written. Line editors also check grammar, consistency, and accuracy of information. Most editors do both acquiring and line editing.

As editor, you are responsible for a book as it moves through all phases of production, and you coordinate the efforts of all other departments. You are also the liaison in house-author relationships.

QUALIFICATIONS

PERSONAL: Love of words and ideas. Creative spirit. A sense of what sells. Tact. Interpersonal skills.

PROFESSIONAL: Excellent command of English. An ability to recognize good writing. Typing (at least 40 words per minute). Familiarity with word processing equipment helpful but not essential. Proofreading skills. Some knowledge of printing and production helpful.

CAREER PATHS

LEVEL	JOB TITLE	EXPERIENCE NEEDED
Entry	Editorial assistant	College degree
2	Assistant or associate editor	1–3 years
3	Senior editor	4–10 years
4	Editorial director	10–15 + years

JOB RESPONSIBILITIES ◆ ENTRY LEVEL

THE BASICS: Answering phones. Doing general clerical work. Checking and routing paperwork.

MORE CHALLENGING DUTIES: Screening unsolicited manuscripts (the slush pile). Writing reports and rejection letters. Writing catalog and jacket copy. Some editing (depending on your assertiveness and your boss's generosity). Solving small problems for authors. Attending editorial meetings.

MOVING UP

In order to move out of the position of glorified secretary, which is what editorial assistants are, you have to prove that you can spot books that are right for your publishing house, know what's needed to improve a manuscript, and work well with temperamental personalities. Being able to convince an author of your judgment is a necessary ingredient to your success.

SALES/MARKETING/ PROMOTION/ADVERTISING

These four related departments are concerned with getting a book into the marketplace and increasing sales in the stores. A hierarchy of sales personnel sell books to jobbers (wholesalers) and retailers. Top people work in-house; the sales representatives work out of their homes or in satellite offices across the country. Many of the smaller publishing houses do not have their own sales reps, or have only a sales manager and one or two field representatives in selected areas. For their sales, they depend on teams of commission representatives, who sell more than one publisher's line. A job as a commission rep is another entry into the business end of book publishing. For the names and addresses of these organizations, consult the *Literary Market Place*.

The marketing staff, which is smaller, promotes the sale of various book lines, series, or individual titles. (Title is the publishing term for an individual book.) They arrange special sales of books to volume buyers outside traditional book outlets, as premiums, gifts, or for special-purpose use. The promotion staff promotes the sales of books in the stores with displays, giveaways, and other devices. They also work to promote the book in the media. Book advertising is limited compared to that of other types of consumer goods, and most is directed to bookstores and libraries.

The sales and business-related staffs must be highly flexible and skilled to handle both large and small campaigns. Many books that are not potential best-sellers do well in the marketplace, and some become strong backlist titles. The backlist is composed of titles that do not have a limited sales life but continue to sell over a long period, and which bookstores must keep in stock. They are an important source of revenue to publishers. Sales and marketing people must come up with ways to support these books that are neither best-sellers nor duds.

If you land an entry-level job in one of the above areas, you'll probably be working as someone's assistant, and your progression from apprentice to management will parallel that of the editorial assistant. The exception is in sales (the largest of the business-related departments), where newcomers start as field representatives and must quickly prove their worth. The following sections describe the sales area.

QUALIFICATIONS

PERSONAL: Outgoing personality. Good conversational skills. Ability to influence others. Follow-through and persistence. Disposition to cope with rejection and not to take the word *No* personally.

PROFESSIONAL: Ability to work comfortably with numbers. Understanding of basic business and management concepts. Sales experience preferred.

CAREER PATHS

LEVEL	JOB TITLE	EXPERIENCE NEEDED
Entry	Sales representative	College degree
2	Regional sales manager	3–7 years
3	Sales manager	10 years

JOB RESPONSIBILITIES ♦ ENTRY LEVEL

THE BASICS: Filing. Doing your own paperwork. Keeping your dealings up to date.

MORE CHALLENGING DUTIES: Visiting stores and wholesalers, presenting book lists. Analyzing the market and your clients. Keeping in contact with the main office.

MOVING UP

After undergoing a brief training period with an experienced sales rep, you will be assigned your own territory. If you work for one of the larger houses, you'll get salary and bonuses and probably even an office. A solid sales record may lead to a position as a regional sales manager in a major marketplace, overseeing the work of sales reps. The few whose administrative and management skills are extraordinary will be promoted to national management positions within the house, overseeing the entire sales operation. Smaller firms have only an overall sales manager. You may work independently or for a separate firm as a commission representative, selling for more than one smaller publisher. In that case, a good sales record can lead to more publishers' lines and a more lucrative territory.

PUBLICITY

The publicity department is responsible for getting authors and their books into the public eye and generating interest in the house's line. A major task is lobbying to get the books reviewed. This department also sends out press releases promoting new books and arranges for author tours and interviews. Author appearances in bookstores, at special events, and at public readings are handled by the publicity department.

QUALIFICATIONS

PERSONAL: Resourcefulness, enthusiasm, and persistence. Good organizational skills. Ability to come up with good ideas. Willingness to follow through.

PROFESSIONAL: Ability to write clear and concise press releases. Good phone manner. Ability to handle details. Typing skills (40 words per minute is the minimum).

CAREER PATHS

LEVEL	JOB TITLE	EXPERIENCE NEEDED
Entry	Publicity assistant	College degree
2	Publicity associate or publicist	2–3 years
3	Publicity director	10 years

JOB RESPONSIBILITIES ♦ ENTRY LEVEL

THE BASICS: Doing general secretarial work. Keeping track of bestseller lists. Making travel arrangements for author tours.

MORE CHALLENGING DUTIES: Attending publicity planning meetings and taking minutes. Reading current house books. Tracking reviews. Following publicity coverage.

MOVING UP

Your training is entirely on the job. Talk to experienced publicists, observe their plans and be prepared to offer your ideas. As a publicist, you will handle entire campaigns and have your own assistants. Building good working relationships with reviewers, magazine editors, and radio and TV people is equally important. The publicity director oversees the department's efforts and may do some or all planning for the top books. Publicity directors who run strong departments are able to influence the size of the budget that any one book or line will get, which requires diplomacy and a strong track record.

PRODUCTION

The production department is responsible for developing the interior and exterior design of the book, choosing paper, determining production costs, and assuring quality. Once pages have been designed and typefaces chosen, production staffers, working with the designer and editor, will select the paper, the method of printing, and the size of the book.

Production is also responsible for getting the finished books to the wholesalers and retailers. Throughout production, a strict schedule must be followed. The greatest challenge is keeping production costs down while maintaining standards of quality.

In breaking into production, a background in layout, printing techniques, and book design is a plus. If your undergraduate major was in a liberal arts major, you might consider taking one or two book publishing production courses, which several universities offer in their extension curriculum.

QUALIFICATIONS

PERSONAL: An eye for detail. An appreciation of books, both in content and form. Good sense of organization.

PROFESSIONAL: Basic understanding of production techniques. Ability to handle figures and budgets. Skill to plan and implement projects lasting many months.

CAREER PATHS

LEVEL	JOB TITLE	EXPERIENCE NEEDED
Entry	Production assistant	College degree
2	Production manager	3–5 years
3	Production director	10 years

JOB RESPONSIBILITIES ♦ ENTRY LEVEL

THE BASICS: Typing. Filing. Handling the stages of a book's production from manuscript through various levels of proof and final readiness to finished book. Following up on schedules with suppliers of materials and services.

MORE CHALLENGING DUTIES: Observing and learning production techniques. Building relationships and suppliers, manufacturers, and free lancers.

MOVING UP

As you begin to understand the production process, you will become more involved in financial management. The key to successful production lies in setting budgets and sticking to them, and large houses may have several staffers who specialize in cost estimation. After reviewing designer specifications, an estimator will determine a particular title's budget for materials and manufacturing. At higher levels, starting with production manager, you are generally responsible for scheduling and assuring that work flows as planned. Production always involves working on several books simultaneously, so this task can be complex. The production director oversees the entire operation and is ultimately responsible for every penny spent.

SUBSIDIARY RIGHTS

In large publishing houses, no more than a half dozen people work in this department, yet subsidiary rights is an important income-generating area. The director and staff license the rights to reuse material from the house's books to magazines and newspapers for serialization; to book clubs and paperback houses for reprint; to theaters, movies, and television for dramatization and performance; and to foreign houses for publication abroad. The rights/permissions assistant, the entry position, handles the flow of contracts and correspondence. Rights' sales add prestige to a book, and the significance of their role in a house's income should not be underestimated. Another perk of subsidiary rights can be travel, if you are responsible for foreign sales.

TEXTBOOK PUBLISHING

Textbooks make more money per year than any other area of publishing, so ample job opportunities exist, primarily for sales reps. Textbooks fall into two categories: el-hi (elementary and high school) and college.

El-hi reps must promote their house's line with school boards, school administrators, state boards of education, and, at times, individual teachers. School contracts often add up to million-dollar sales and may last for years, so competition is fierce and reps must know their product well and be enthusiastic about it in order to clinch deals. Field reps also play a role in making sure their publishers know about trends in various subject areas so they reflect them in their textbooks.

College textbook publishing often holds more appeal to recent college graduates because it's a way to stay involved with university life. Sales reps in this area are known as college travelers. You don't need a degree in a particular major to sell texts in it, but you will need some knowledge of that area in order to sell effectively.

As a traveler, you'll be assigned to visit campuses and meet with professors in a specific geographical area. Besides selling, you may acquire new titles or recruit academics to write or contribute to a new textbook. College travelers often get house and author together.

You'll find the same basic functional areas in textbook houses that exist in trade houses. Experience on the road is a good starting point from which to move into virtually any area. The key to success in all phases of the textbook industry is a clear understanding of the ever-changing educational marketplace, and such experience is only gained through time spent as a field representative.

ADDITIONAL INFORMATION

SALARIES

Publishing salaries vary widely depending on the size and type of the house and an individual's experience. Textbook publishers usually pay better than trade publishers. In general, publishing salaries fall into the following ranges.

EDITORIAL

Editorial assistant	$13,000 to 19,000
Assistant editor	$16,000 to 20,000
Senior editor [Managing editor]	$33,000 to 40,000
Editorial director [Executive editor]	$43,000 to 50,000

SALES

Sales representative	$19,000 to 28,000 plus commission
Sales manager	$30,000 to 75,000

PUBLICITY

Publicity assistant	$17,000 to 20,000
Publicist	$18,000 to 24,000
Publicity director	$25,000 to 50,000

PRODUCTION

Production assistant	$14,000 to 18,000
Production manager	$22,000 to 40,000
Production director	$35,000 to 50,000

WORKING CONDITIONS

HOURS: Ten to six are normal working hours in editorial, although as an assistant, you will probably have to show up at nine to cover the phones. Plan on taking reading home from the beginning if you're ambitious. In sales, you'll be working whenever the clients can see you, which is usually, although not always, during business hours. Paperwork is often done outside the nine-to-five period. In publicity, you'll be placing plenty of calls to the West Coast (where there are many media outlets), which, if you're on the East Coast, can mean working between six and nine in the evening (the afternoon working hours for Californians) when you're handling an especially important campaign.

ENVIRONMENT: Only the largest publishing houses have working space that can be called comfortable, although after a few years you'll be given a cubbyhole office of your own.

WORKSTYLE: In addition to clerical work, much of your time as an editorial assistant will be spent reading. You'll also be on the phone frequently, getting in touch with authors and tracking down information for your editor. Eventually, you'll be invited to meetings where new projects and the progress of others is discussed. In sales, you'll spend much of your time out of the office, making calls on book buyers, both in bookstores and in warehouse surroundings. When you're not making calls, you'll be in the office, setting up appointments for them by phone. As a publicity person, you'll spend much of your day on the telephone with media contacts arranging interviews for the authors you represent. Count on plenty of paperwork, too; calls must be preceded by a letter, press release, or copy of the book. In production, your time will be absorbed dealing with people—designers, typesetters, printers—much of it over the phone.

TRAVEL: Only senior editors travel to conferences or the twice-yearly sales conference. In sales you'll be traveling on a regular basis, covering the area assigned to you, which may be as small as several big city neighborhoods or as large as several less densely populated states. Travel opportunities are extremely limited for those in publicity, production, and subsidiary rights.

EXTRACURRICULAR ACTIVITIES/WORK EXPERIENCE

College literary magazine—contributing, copy editing, editing, doing production and distribution

Campus or local bookstore—working as a sales clerk or book buyer

Campus publications (newspaper, magazine, yearbook)—reporting, writing, editing, proofreading, doing layout and production, selling space

Student activities office (for publicity work)—planning, coordinating, promoting entertainment and lecture events

Regional literary publications—working as an editorial or business management assistant

Student-initiated publication projects of any kind—done as classroom projects, extracurricular, or professional efforts

INTERNSHIPS

There are no formal internships in book publishing, although you may be able to set one up on your own by contacting the head of the department of the house for which you'd like to work.

RECOMMENDED READING

BOOKS

Against the Grain: Interviews with Maverick American Publishers, Robert Dana, ed., University of Iowa Press: 1986

An Introduction to Book Publishing by D. Raghavan, Apt. Books: 1988

Between Covers: The Rise and Transformation of Book Publishing in America by John William Tebbel, Oxford University Press: 1987

Book Publishing Career Directory, Ron Fry, ed., Career Press Inc.: 1987

The Huenefeld Guide to Book Publishing by John Huenefeld, 3rd. rev. ed., Huenefeld Company: 1986

International Literary Market Place, R. R. Bowker Company: 1984 (directory of publishers, major booksellers and libraries, agents and other people and organizations associated with the book trade in 160 countries)

The Literary Market Place, R. R. Bowker Company: 1984 (directory of U.S. and Canadian book publishers and all associated individuals and organizations, with addresses and phone numbers)

Opportunities in Book Publishing Careers by Robert A. Carter, National Textbook Company: 1987

So Far so Good: Recollections of a Life in Publishing by Edwin Seaver, Chicago Review: 1987

Stet! Tricks of the Trade for Writers and Editors, Bruce O. Boston, ed., Editorial Experts: 1986

PERIODICALS
American Bookseller (monthly), Booksellers Publishing, Inc., 122 East 42nd Street, New York, NY 10168

Publishers Weekly (weekly), R. R. Bowker Company, 245 West 17th Street, New York, NY 10011

Library Journal (bimonthly), R. R. Bowker Company, 245 West 17th Street, New York, NY 10011

Small Press: The Magazine of Independent In-House Desktop Publishing, Meckler Publishing Corp., 11 Ferry Lane West, Westport, CT 06880

PROFESSIONAL ASSOCIATIONS

American Booksellers Association
122 East 42nd Street
New York, NY 10169

Association of American Publishers
1 Park Avenue
New York, NY 10016

Children's Book Council, Inc.
67 Irving Place
New York, NY 10003

Publisher's Publicity Association
200 Madison Avenue
New York, NY 10016

Women's National Book Association, Inc.
106 Fifth Avenue
New York, NY 10010

INTERVIEWS

JOSH GASPERO
PUBLISHER
JOSHUA MORRIS, INC.
WESTPORT, CT

My publishing career actually started in the chocolate business. After graduating from college, I spent two years in the Peace Corps, got an M.B.A. and went into sales with Hershey. I wound up as a product manager who had ambitions to do something more creative than changing candy packaging, so I put together the *Hershey 1934 Cookbook*. It helped Hershey increase sales and provided an outlet for my fascination with the printed word.

Then I decided to set up my own consulting business to advise clients on the international confectionery business and publishing. As so often happens, I was hired by one of the companies I dealt with, Western Publishing in Racine, WI. I started as marketing manager and within five years was the vice president of sales and marketing for all of Western's books. By then I was ready for another change, so when the opportunity to become president of another company presented itself, I moved to Ideals Publishing Corporation, which was owned by Harlequin Books. I subsequently became president of a second subsidiary—a magazine group which included *Ideals*, *Art News*, and *Antiques World*.

I went on to become president of Harlequin Books, which is based in Toronto. After two years, I finally decided to come to New York City. It is the mecca of publishing, and your chances of success are better here, especially if you're young. With a partner, Michael Morris, I started a publishing company called Joshua Morris in 1983. Together we have 40 years of experience in publishing and contacts around the world. We know international publishing, an area where few people have expertise.

Currently we take children's books from abroad and publish them in the United States. My partner and I decided to begin by acquiring the rights to previously published books, because starting from scratch—dealing with authors, editors, and artists—takes time. As we grow, our plan is to develop our own books and have our own list of original titles.

I believe whatever you publish must entertain. For example, Harlequin romances are not great literature, but people like them, and they are not bad, editorially or morally. Romances are not my taste, but I wouldn't hesitate to let my daughter read them.

Harlequin has been called the "McDonald's of publishing."

That's not a bad analogy; both companies turn out a quality product which is marketed well. To me the process of publishing a book is intriguing, as long as the product is good. You don't have to be a dyed-in-the-wool bibliophile to be in publishing, but you must know and respect books.

Publishing is a tough business, with one of the worst returns on investments of any industry. I think it's best to approach a book like a product. You should know what you can spend on it, have a marketing strategy, and calculate what you can expect to earn. Publishing is now a consumer products business. To be successful, you've got to appeal to the public and publish what it wants. I also believe you can apply business discipline to publishing without sacrificing the creative process.

ADAM ROTHBERG
SENIOR PUBLICIST
POCKET BOOKS
NEW YORK, NY

I started in publishing four and a half years ago. This was my first serious job out of college, so I came in on the ground floor as the assistant to the director of publicity. Since I wanted a position in the area of creative communications, I chose publicity within the publishing field. I love reading and I love books so this seemed a natural fit to me.

I arrived the first day very green, with no office experience and no knowledge of office protocol. I had to learn the ropes; the most basic skills including how to take a proper phone message.

A year later I was promoted to assistant-publicist and with that came more responsibility. Three and a half years later I moved through the ranks to my current position as senior-publicist.

My job requires lots of contact with all kinds of people: authors, producers, reporters from radio, tv and newspapers, and the people in the sales and editorial divisions of my company.

The heart of the business is to make books known within the industry and to the public. This is accomplished by booking radio and TV spots, setting-up interviews, and concentrating on getting books reviewed. There's a lot of variety and this makes the job fun.

We publish over 300 books per month so not all the titles get the same amount of attention. At the very least a book gets a press release. There are also book parties and autographing sessions.

Pocket Books publishes something for everyone: sports books, novels, literary fiction, adventure fiction. Some of the more famous books and authors: *Slaves of New York*, Tama Janowitz; *A Season on the Brink*, John Fienstein; *Red Army*, Ralph Peters.

Since you get to cut your teeth on different types of products, there's always a new challenge. Your approach will depend on the position of the book. You need to cultivate a whole new set of contacts for each type of book you promote. Also the type of promotions vary from product to product. For example media bookings usually don't work for fiction.

The job requires a lot of creative thinking. You're always looking for new ways of getting books noticed above and beyond traditional means. If I'm working with a war book, a military affairs writer for a newspaper may be more interested in interviewing the author than a traditional book reviewer. There are lots of books and authors going around, and the name of the game is getting attention.

An important characteristic to have in this business is a thick skin. You will hear no more than you hear yes. There is a lot of rejection. Be persistent; persevere. People are hard to reach; you may keep missing them. Then at the very last minute you reach them and get a yes. You'll be on the phone a lot so good phone skills are a must.

Diplomacy and tact are also important. Often you'll have to juggle the needs and desires of the company, the author, and the producers you are trying to convince to help promote your product.

Good writing skills are key as a publicist. Time and care need to be taken for writing creative press releases and other materials because what you write may determine whether or not a book gets attention. Famous authors will carry their own weight but lesser known authors will rely more on the help of a well constructed press release.

Get connected with the Publishers Publicist Association. This is an independent non-profit group that is an excellent job source on the entry level. You can confidentially submit a résumé and they have people who recruit entry-level people. It's also a good place for workshops and seminars for people already in the field.

When you first get started you have to put up with a lot of grunt work before the exciting projects happen. It's an underpaid industry but if you stick with it the rewards can be satisfying. Just recently, I got my first interview with *Newsweek* and I was walking on air all week.

AMY LEHN
ASSOCIATE EDITOR
JOHN WILEY & SONS, EDUCATIONAL GROUP
NEW YORK, NY

I graduated from college with a marketing degree and wanted to do something related. I began with a position at Milady publishing company, a small family owned company, as a marketing assistant. There was not a great deal of growth so when Milady was acquired by John Wiley in 1985, I moved to Wiley as a sales assistant.

Two years later an assistant editor's job opened. I did not have an editorial background or an English background but I was aware of the books in the division and easily moved into the position. One year later I was promoted to associate editor and took on two additional lines.

My line consists of 15 real estate, 5 math and 2 physics titles. There are no specific acquiring and developing editors in our division so a lot of those responsibilities are mine.

Part of my job includes traveling with the reps looking for

authors. When I find an author, the manuscript or a writing sample is sent out to reviewers. Research is done to assess the market; decide on content; what should be added and deleted; how the book flows and if it follows a course outline.

If the reviews are favorable a contract is drawn up and the author sends in 3 to 4 chapters at a time. These chapters are then sent to reviewers and the developmental process continues until the book is completed.

I see the project from manuscript through production. I handle the budget, the cover design, how long the book should be, even what kind of paper to use, every detail. Production then deals with the author once all of these decisions are made.

I also work with marketing, deciding on whether or not there should be a promotional letter or brochure for the book. I give information to the reps; what is the target market, what are the features, how does it differ from the competition, what is the pricing?

My favorite part of the job is the diversity. I am called on to make creative decisions as well as concrete ones regarding pricing and production. I also interact with other editors, the field reps and the authors.

For example I just got back from California where we visited several teachers who are using our books. This was a fact finding mission to discuss why they purchased the book; what they would change; and generally their opinion of the product. This input is important if we are going into another edition and also to help fine tune a particular marketing strategy.

My job always has me writing and speaking with authors, marketing people, clients, production. It's important to have a good sense of written and verbal communications and to develop sound working relationships. You must be precise in conveying what you want.

A good course for those going into trade book publishing is New York University's *Introduction to Book Publishing*. This course takes you through all the aspects of producing a book, so you can get an idea of which way to go: marketing, editorial, or production.

I would also recommend any of the time management programs on how to structure your day and how to prioritize. These are important skills in any industry.

BROADCASTING

I t's only natural that the broadcasting industry be a popular career choice among those entering the job market. After all, radio has been a firmly established part of American life since the 1930s, and anyone who has come of age in the past 40 years has spent a great many hours glued to the tube.

Although the broadcasting industry is huge, it continues to grow. About 10,500 radio stations now broadcast in this country, with about 200 new stations hitting the airwaves each year. In the TV business the arrival of cable TV has sparked a tremendous change in an industry that, ironically, itself served as a major revolutionary force in both communications and society in general. Prior to cable TV, the business was dominated by the three major networks, CBS, NBC, and ABC. Now, more than 100 different specialty services, networks, and "superstations" are vying for the attention of the more than 50 million households wired for cable service.

All this diversification and growth is good news for viewers and listeners. It's even better news for those hoping to forge a career in broadcasting—television in particular. Cable TV executives realize they can only go so far with rehashed reruns and faded flicks. To keep viewers, they have to offer something worth watching. They need programming.

With all those radio and TV stations, it would seem that jobs would be available for the asking. The fact is, however, that competition is indeed keen. Most broadcasting professionals get their start in small, sometimes out-of-the-way, stations and markets. It's only after years of leapfrogging to slightly better jobs in slightly bigger markets that most broadcasting professionals land their dream job. Many settle for roles in smaller stations.

Any skills, experience, or knowledge you can bring with you will be of immense help. If your primary target is broadcast journalism, for instance, a journalism degree or minor is almost a must, and an advanced degree in political science or international studies can certainly help. Experience on a college radio station can actually count for more than an advanced degree.

In TV, ground-floor experience is more attainable than in the past. Many local cable systems feature independent stations of their own. These stations are typically run on little or no budget, and the programming can be less than exhilarating, but the experience counts. At a smaller station, you're likely to get a shot at some valuable hands-on work.

JOB OUTLOOK

JOB OPENINGS WILL GROW: As fast as average in radio; faster than average in TV.

COMPETITION FOR JOBS: Keen

NEW JOB OPORTUNITIES: Syndicated radio services, which provide and distribute a wide array of recorded programs, continue to grow in number and importance. Westwood One, which has grown since its inception in the mid-1970s to become a significant force in radio is one of the biggest syndicators. In TV, there are more than 100 different channels and services vying for the attention of cable viewers. That number is likely to stay strong, as more and more American homes are wired for cable.

GEOGRAPHIC JOB INDEX

The corporate offices of both radio and TV networks are in New York, NY, and Los Angeles, CA. New York is the home of the news bureaus and most daytime soap operas, whereas the majority of network entertainment programming originates on the West Coast. Important network television desks also operate in Chicago, IL, and Washington, DC. However, most job openings exist outside these centers, in local broadcasting.

WHO THE EMPLOYERS ARE

MAJOR TELEVISION NETWORKS (ABC, CBS, NBC) employ thousands in their corporate offices, but job opportunities there are extremely limited for recent grads. An entry-level job at a network often requires the applicant to have professional experience or an advanced degree in business or law. Other jobs for recent graduates are usually secretarial or of the go-fer variety. Advancement is possible but difficult.

COMMERCIAL TELEVISION STATIONS operate across the country; there are approximately 1000 such stations. The networks each have about 200 affiliates; some are directly owned by the parent network, others operate independently. In either case, each affiliate has its own hiring policies and procedures, as do the country's 415 independent stations.

NATIONAL RADIO NETWORKS (ABC, CBS, NBC) provide programming for their affiliate stations and, along with the other major networks—the Mutual Broadcasting System, AP Radio Network, UPI Audio, and RKO Radio Network—provide extensive coverage of national and international events and a variety of features to member stations.

STATE OR REGIONAL RADIO NETWORKS are associations of broadcast stations within a state or region that supply news of that area to member stations. These networks are the Florida News Network, Texas State Network, Oklahoma News Network, and the Arkansas, Georgia, Louisiana, Mississippi, and Missouri Networks.

The goal of many graduates is to land a job in one of the

approximately 50 major television markets, which serve at least 500,000 viewing households, or the 25 largest U.S. cities that have a population of at least 1,300,000 and make up the major radio markets. Major market stations attract top-level, experienced people. Competition for the relatively few entry-level jobs is intense.

MEDIUM AND SMALL MARKET RADIO STATIONS are located throughout the country. Cities with populations of between 500,000 and 1,000,000 are considered medium markets. Small market radio stations are found in communities of under 50,000, and nearly 40 percent of all radio stations in the United States fall into this latter category.

INDEPENDENT RADIO SYNDICATORS produce and distribute programming. Most of this production is music, but news, sports, and other features are also packaged. These services provide job opportunities primarily for graduates interested in programming and production.

PUBLIC TELEVISION STATIONS, numbering 339, make up the PBS system. The deliver educational, information, and artistic programming and operate in 49 states (all but Montana) and four U.S. territories, making PBS the world's most extensive television system. Each station does its own hiring, and staff size depends on the amount of production done at the station. However, very few public stations have the personnel or resources required for extensive production, so most PBS programming originates from the following five stations: WGBH (Boston, MA), WNET (New York, NY), WETA (Washington, DC), KCET (Los Angeles, CA), and WTTW (Chicago, IL). PBS headquarters in Washington, DC, is a small operation and employs primarily administrative staff. The radio counterpart of PBS is National Public Radio, with more than 180 stations across the United States. Here, too, hiring is done by individual stations, and programming is generated to the extent that station resources will allow. Other programming—such as NPR's

"Morning Edition" and "All Things Considered"—comes from their Washington, DC, headquarters.

MAJOR EMPLOYERS

The eight largest U.S. television broadcast markets, those with more than 1,500,000 viewing households, are listed here in order of size. Each of these cities also has a number of independent stations in addition to the network affiliates and PBS stations listed below.

1. NEW YORK, NY
AFFILIATE: WABC (ABC), WCBS (CBS), WNBC (NBC)
PBS: WNET, WNYC

2. LOS ANGELES, CA
AFFILIATE: KABC (ABC), KNBC (NBC), KCBC (CBS)
PBS: KCET, KLCS

3. CHICAGO, IL
AFFILIATE: WBBM (CBS), WLS (ABC), WMAQ (NBC)
PBS: WTTW

4. PHILADELPHIA, PA
AFFILIATE: KYW (NBC), WCAU (CBS), WPVI (ABC)
PBS: WHYY

5. SAN FRANCISCO, CA
AFFILIATE: KGO (ABC), KPIX (CBS), KRON (NBC)
PBS: KQED, KQEC

6. BOSTON, MA
AFFILIATE: WBZ (NBC), WCBV (ABC), WNEV (CBS)
PBS: WGBH

7. DETROIT, MI
AFFILIATE: WDIV (NBC), WJBK (CBS), WXYZ (ABC)
PBS: WTVS

8. DALLAS–FORT WORTH, TX
AFFILIATE: KDFW (CBS), KFAA (ABC), KXAS (NBC)
PBS: KERA

The following cities are the top 25 radio markets, which each have at least 1,300,000 listeners.

1. New York, NY
2. Los Angeles, CA
3. Chicago, IL
4. San Francisco, CA
5. Philadelphia, PA
6. Detroit, MI
7. Boston, MA
8. Dallas–Ft. Worth, TX
9. Washington, DC
10. Houston–Galveston, TX
11. Hollywood, CA
12. Nassau–Suffolk, NY
13. Atlanta, GA
14. Seattle–Tacoma, WA
15. St. Louis, MO
16. Pittsburgh, PA
17. Baltimore, MD
18. Minneapolis–St. Paul, MN
19. San Diego, CA
20. Anaheim–Santa Ana, CA
21. Cleveland, OH
22. Tampa–St. Petersburg, FL
23. Phoenix, AZ
24. Denver–Boulder, CO
25. Portland, OR

HOW TO BREAK INTO THE FIELD

Knowing someone who can hire you or tell you about openings and recommend you is your best bet, but prior experience is the key.

Investigate internship opportunities at a local station, or volunteer to work during summers and weekends. (Public television and radio stations are often the most receptive to volunteer help.) And get involved with your campus radio or TV station. Your best chance for a first job is at a small station. Send a carefully thought-out and well-written letter to the general manager of the station you've chosen and request an interview. Follow up with a phone call.

The once-rapid growth in programming services for the cable television industry slowed somewhat in 1983. Some services proved to be unprofitable and have folded or merged with more successful ones. Job openings, where they do occur, are often taken by experienced professionals. If you are willing to work part-time or as a free lancer instead of waiting for a staff opening, you may stand a chance of finding a job in this area.

Most large radio stations hold newswriting examinations, which applicants have likened to taking the bar exam. The writer is given two hours to go over 12 hours worth of wire copy and create a five-minute radio newscast from it. Such an exam should not be undertaken until you have a considerable amount of experience under your belt.

If you're female, or a member of a minority group, you can get help in finding positions in commercial broadcasting by writing to:

NAB Employment Clearinghouse
1771 N Street, N.W.
Washington, DC 20036

If you'd like to work in public radio, the National Association of Educational Broadcasters operates PACT (People and Careers in Telecommunications), a free, nationwide employment service. Write to:

National Association of Educational Broadcasters PACT
1346 Connecticut Avenue, N.W.
Washington, DC 20036

Competition for on-air jobs in both radio and television is intense. Hopefuls must have not only good reporting skills, but a clear speaking voice, an attractive appearance (for television), and an appealing presence as well. Starting in a small market is a must. Advancement comes by moving to larger and larger markets, and only the very best make it to the network level.

Much more plentiful are behind-the-scenes reporting jobs: writing and editing copy, preparing background research, and keeping and updating files on developing stories. These jobs can be just as exciting and demanding as those of reporters and anchors and provide better stepping-stones to management positions.

BROADCASTING ENTREPRENEURIAL

Starting your own TV station may be out of the question—unless your name is Ted Turner or Rupert Murdoch—but the TV business does offer exciting opportunites to budding entrepreneurs.

One of the potentially more lucrative channels is in video production. As part of the deal that local cable outlets strike with cable programming services, the local companies are allowed a certain amount of air time to sell to area businesses during a cablecast. Most local advertisers are smaller businesses that don't have the resources to hire their own production crews. They rely on independent production houses to film their commercials. People who have put some time into the TV production business have gone on to start successful independent enterprises.

NEWS

By far the best opportunities for political science or history majors in broadcasting exist in radio and television news departments. The news department is often the largest at a station, but job opportunities are often awarded first to those with a journalism background. However, here your background may give you a competitive edge.

Radio news departments receive national and international news over a teletype machine from the news services: Associated Press (AP) and United Press International (UPI). Less frequently the news is sent as an audio feed by broadcast lines to local stations.

For local stories, the stations fend for themselves. Armed with a tape recorder and microphone, their reporters go wherever the action is. As a reporter, you'll interview people at the scene, take notes, and tape-record interviews and meetings before writing a story summarizing the event and editing the tape for appropriate quotes to thread into your story. You'll write, edit, and deliver the story back at the station if there's still time before the next newscast; otherwise you'll write the story on the spot and dictate if over the phone into a machine at the station.

Most radio stations broadcast the news at least once every hour. Although news jobs are extremely difficult to get, the total number of these jobs has increased because of the growing number of stations broadcasting "all news" 24 hours a day.

QUALIFICATIONS

PERSONAL: Natural curiosity. A capacity for hard work and long hours. Ability to handle pressure and deadlines. For on-air work, good diction. A voice and delivery that convey warmth and authority.

PROFESSIONAL: Television: Reporting and writing skills. Typing required; knowledge of video display terminals (VDTs) helpful, as these are becoming more common in TV newsrooms. Ability to work accurately with speed, usually under pressure of a deadline.

RADIO: Ability to write for the ear. Sound news judgment. Good reporting, editing, and rewriting skills. Ability to edit tape.

CAREER PATHS

TELEVISION: (These apply primarily to off-camera personnel.)

LEVEL	JOB TITLE	EXPERIENCE NEEDED
Entry	Desk assistant	College degree
2	Newswriter	1–2 years
3	Assistant news producer	6–8 years
4	News producer	10–12 years

RADIO

LEVEL	JOB TITLE	EXPERIENCE NEEDED
Entry	Desk assistant, network radio	College degree
	Reporter, small network	
2	Reporter, medium market	2 years
3	Reporter, major market	5 years
	News director, small market	
4	News director, major market	10+ years
	Reporter, network	

JOB RESPONSIBILITIES ♦ ENTRY LEVEL

THE BASICS: Clerical duties. Maintaining news service machines. Collecting and distributing audio feeds to news editors and writers. Helping prepare sports scores and weather round-ups. Checking facts. General messenger duties for the news department.

MORE CHALLENGING DUTIES: Television: Writing or rewriting copy. Simple editing of copy to conform to time limitations. Reviewing film clips. Radio: Interviewing sources. Putting together an early morning newscast by clearing the news wire machines on copy that has "moved" during the night and pulling stories for use on the upcoming newscasts, listening to audio feeds, phoning police and hospitals for overnight news and updates, then writing and editing the newscast from the material gathered.

MOVING UP

As an assistant, you learn the daily routine of the newsroom, the style of its scripted copy, and the discipline to write under deadline. Once you reach the level of newswriter, you write the actual copy and you may edit other writers' stories. In radio, your next job will no doubt be reporting.

Several years of writing or reporting experience may lead to the position of assistant news producer in television, which combines organizational and managerial skills with critical judgment. In radio, a promotion possibility is becoming a news director, if you've proved yourself to be an ace reporter and, in addition, have managerial know-how. At most radio stations, the news director determines the overall news policy of the station, supervises the news personnel, and previews the newscasts to ensure that they're a satisfying blend of local, national, and international concerns. The news director also may serve as a reporter and newscaster.

In television, the assistant news producer, in cooperation with the news producer, oversees the daily routine, assigns stories, and decides which stories get precedence. These senior people also have the last word in the selection of accompanying film.

PROGRAMMING-PRODUCTION

Because the networks are responsible for the majority of daytime and evening programming, their program staffs number in the hundreds. Major programming areas beyond the news and documentary departments—sports, morning talk shows, soap operas, children's programs, and prime-time shows—have individual staffs. The television network programming and production staffs conceive, plan, and create most shows except for prime-time shows and made-for-TV movies, which they commission or purchase from independent production houses. In radio, all on-air material except for news is selected, prepared, or purchased by the programming department. Independent and network-affiliate TV stations still do a sizable amount of programming themselves, and this is where many job openings can be found. In radio, FCC regulations oblige the station to provide public service programming, and this may well be a place where your background is particularly apt. In addition, the surging popularity of talk shows has increased the number of people needed to plan and produce that type of programming. In fact, a growing number of major AM stations have become all-talk, and most stations do at least some talk show programming that is often aired early on Sunday mornings or late on Sunday evenings. Hosting a show, lining up guests, and developing a formula for talk programming is often the job of the director of public affairs. Although you may be given one of these responsibilities at a small station on your first job, you'll have to become more seasoned in programming before going on to a similar position at a medium or major market station.

Production staffers may develop program ideas, prepare scripts, work with free lance writers and on-air talent, and edit the show after taping. In radio, if you're a talented behind-the scenes programming person, you could be hired as an associate producer, helping the producer to conceive, develop, and produce a show; conducting interviews; writing scripts; and editing tapes. If you demonstrate taste and can forecast trends, you'll be ready to move up to producer, a position in which you'll choose the people to be interviewed, handle all the business arrangements, supervise production personnel, and act as overall manager of the program. Success in any of these areas may land you a job as program director, responsible for coordinating and presenting the complete daily programming schedule.

The television production assistant is, in many ways, an apprentice. Opportunities for advancement depend on the size of the station and the complexity of its operations. As assistant producer, you might work on a specific regular program or on various specials. You typically then become a producer, working in ever larger markets on more involved programming. Or you might move on to an administrative position, such as production director or program director.

ADDITIONAL INFORMATION

SALARIES

Network people make the highest salaries. At both independent and network-affiliated stations, the larger the market, the higher the pay. Those who work in public television or radio make less than their counterparts at commercial stations. The following figures, compiled by the National Association of Broadcasters in a recent survey, represent the average salary nationwide.

RADIO

News editor	$20,185
News reporter	$17,028
News announcer	$19,450
News director	$20,144

TELEVISION

News reporter	$26,152
News producer	$24,919
News anchor	$55,607

WORKING CONDITIONS

HOURS: Radio: Many radio stations operate 24 hours a day, seven days a week, so in news expect to work long hours. As a neophyte, you'll often be assigned the worst shifts (midnight to 8 A.M.; 4:30

A.M. to noon), and to weekend and holiday assignments. Be prepared for overtime. Television: News must be reported up until the end of the 11 P.M. newscast seven days a week, and into the early hours on the networks' late-night programs.

ENVIRONMENT: In general, the atmosphere is noisy, cluttered, and hectic, with ringing phones and loud talk. Office privacy is a luxury reserved for senior staff members. Because reporters are under continuous deadline pressure, it's a high-tension, fast-moving atmosphere.

WORKSTYLE: As a reporter, you're on your feet and out of the office much of the day, tracking down stories. The rest of the time you're in the newsroom editing and rewriting stories that come in over the wires.

TRAVEL: Only network-level reporters do a significant amount of out-of-town travel, and they are usually based in major cities or even abroad.

EXTRACURRICULAR ACTIVITIES/WORK EXPERIENCE

Campus newspaper, publications, radio or television station—reporting and writing, production, announcing
Volunteer—local public radio or television station
Sports events—announcing
Drama club—directing, acting, technical crew
Debate club—participant

INTERNSHIPS

The International Radio and Television Society's internship program is open only to junior and senior communications majors. Investigate summer and part-time opportunities by contacting local radio and television stations and cable systems. Although some stations pay interns, most take them only as volunteers.

RECOMMENDED READING

BOOKS

Bad News at Black Rock: The Sellout of CBS News, by Peter McCabe, Arbor House: 1987

Breaking into Broadcasting: Getting a Good Job in Radio or T.V., Out Front or Behind the Scenes, by Donn Pearlman, Bonus Books: 1986

The Broadcaster's Dictionary, Wind River Books: 1987

The Broadcaster's Survival Guide, by Jack W. Whitley and Gregg F. Skall, Pharos Books: 1988

Broadcasting Yearbook, published by Broadcasting Publications, Inc. (lists names and addresses of radio stations, national and regional networks, and major program producers)

Hold On, Mr. President by Sam Donaldson, Random House: 1987

International Handbook of Broadcasting Systems, by Philip T. Rosen, Greenwood: 1988

It Only Hurts When I Laugh, by Stan Freberg, Times Books: 1988

Skills for Radio Broadcasters, by Curtis Holsopple, 3rd ed., TAB Books: 1987

PERIODICALS

Billboard (weekly), Billboard Publications, 1 Astor Plaza, 1515 Broadway, New York, NY 10036

Broadcasting (weekly), Broadcasting Publications, Inc., 1735 DeSales Street, N.W., Washington, DC 20036

Cable Television Business (weekly), Cardiff Publishing Company, 6430 Yosemite Street, Englewood, CO 80111

Inside TV (monthly), McFadden Holdings, 215 Lexington Avenue, New York, NY 10016

Radio & Records (weekly), 1930 Century Park West, Los Angeles, CA 90067

Television Radio Age (biweekly), Television Editorial Corp., 1270 Avenue of the Americas, New York, NY 10020

Variety (weekly), Variety, Inc., 154 West 46th Street, New York, NY 10036

PROFESSIONAL ASSOCIATIONS

American Women in Radio and Television
1321 Connecticut Avenue, N.W.
Washington, DC 20036

International Radio and Television Society
420 Lexington Avenue
New York, NY 10170

The National Association of Broadcasters
1771 N Street, N.W.
Washington, DC 20036

The National Radio Broadcasters Association
1705 DeSales Street, N.W.
Washington, DC 20036

INTERVIEWS

ROVING CORRESPONDENT
ABC RADIO NEWS
NEW YORK, NY

Although I majored in journalism in college, I never took a broadcasting course. I didn't even work at the campus radio station. I was too shy to speak in front of a microphone—or so I thought until I got my first job at a small FM station in Sylvania, OH. I worked as a disc jockey and a news broadcaster there before I was named news director for a larger station, WIOT, in Ohio.

As news director at major stations in Cincinnati, Philadelphia, and Chicago, I've covered five national political conventions, White House news conferences, the emergency at Three Mile Island, the visits of the Pope, the Winter Olympics, the World Series, and the Super Bowl.

For several years, I worked the morning drive shift (6 to 10 A.M.). It's difficult to be creative, funny, and compelling on the air at an early hour. But that's the time when most people want their daily dose of news. When you have to get up at four o'clock in the morning, your social life is terrible.

It took me 11 years to land the radio job of my dreams—working as a roving correspondent for ABC News—but it was worth it. Had I been tied down with a relationship or marriage, I might not have been able to relocate as often as I did, which is what most people in my business do in order to move up to bigger and better markets.

I think I have the greatest job in radio news. I go wherever a big story or event is happening, and I get to tell it to hundreds of thousands of young Americans. While most of the stories I work on are exciting, I'm also required to be on the scene whenever necessary, which may mean showing up at 8 A.M. to cover a story on dioxin contamination in Hoboken, NJ.

If you want to work in radio, get as much firsthand experience as you can while you're still in school, at the campus station or a local one. Take a wide variety of courses so you're knowledgeable about many subjects. And be persistent in your search to get into a radio news slot. It's competitive, but if you're willing to start out at a small station and build on your experience, you're bound to go places.

DIRECTOR OF GRANT SUPPORT
PUBLIC TELEVISION STATION

The highlights of my job are selling a quality product and working with people who really enjoy their work. I'm surrounded by very bright people who want to be here. There's a team spirit at our station that I have never known on other jobs.

I'm responsible for finding corporate sponsors or underwriters for programs my station produces for national delivery through PBS. My clients are high-level corporate people, usually close to senior vice presidential level. To them, I'm not so much a salesman as I am a broker, bringing two interested parties together. My job is to travel to cities where corporate headquarters are located to see if I can interest them in associating their names with a production. Usually, their company has expressed interest in public television, and my job is to find the right product for them. I talk frequently with our programming department to try to match up something that's in the works with a particular company's needs.

I like to define our product as the Rolls-Royce of TV programming. Those of us in public television see ourselves as part of a widely accepted alternative to standard and predictable commercial fare. We make less money than our counterparts in network or local TV. However in my department, there's more opportunity than in others to earn a good living because we're paid on a salary plus commission basis.

DEPARTMENT STORE RETAILING

Consumers generally take for granted that they will always find their favorite department stores brimming with merchandise. Unnoticed by most customers, a large, talented staff works long, hard hours to keep the shelves filled, the selection varied, the stores beautiful, and the business of retailing running smoothly. Retailing is an industry in which brains and diligence can take you to high levels of decision-making years before your contemporaries in other fields have reached similar positions of responsibility.

Graduates of virtually any discipline may enter department store retailing. Prospective employers are looking for demonstrated capacity to learn and make quick, sound judgments and are less interested in academic backgrounds. You must be flexible, comfortable with people, self-disciplined, and highly motivated—and a sense of humor certainly does not hurt. Retailing is a high-pressure profession where no slow seasons exist—only busy and busier, with the November-December pre-Christmas rush being the most hectic time of all. Prior retail experience, even a summer spent behind a cash register, is a plus; some retailers won't consider candidates without it.

Department store chains, once noted for their consistency and stability, have been caught up in the whirlwind of corporate mergers and takeovers that has been sweeping across the American business landscape since the mid-1980s. Many of the most recognizable names in the business—B. Altman, Bloomingdale's, Bonwit Teller, and Abraham and Straus, among others—have changed ownership at least once, as retail-chain conglomerates like Federated Department Stores and Allied Stores shuffle and reshuffle their holdings. No less a pillar of business than Sears Roebuck, a fixture in American society since the dawn of the 20th century, has remolded itself to keep pace with its competition.

A big reason for this instability, of course, is the rise of the shopping mall. Multiple-store malls are now ubiquitous in most areas of the country. For the most part, these malls consist of one or two large department stores and a host of smaller specialty shops and boutiques. The competition from smaller shops has become increasingly intense. Although smaller stores can't match the big chains when it comes to variety and price, by specializing they can lure customers away. For this reason, many chains have abandoned the practice of offering steady but predictable merchandise in favor of infusing more creativity into the sales process. To do this, they need creative people who have a good idea about what customers want and how to present it.

Most entry-level jobs are in merchandising, an area further divided into:

◆ **STORE MANAGEMENT**

◆ **BUYING**

The talents of the art major are specifically in demand in two small, specialized job areas:

◆ **FASHION COORDINATION**

◆ **DISPLAY**

Fashion coordination is a job area found only in larger stores; neither job area employs a large staff, but both areas require a strong creative flair.

Most entry-level jobs are in merchandising. Your job in merchandising begins with a training period of six months to a year. Some trainees divide their time between classroom learning and work experience, others train entirely on the job. Generally, the larger the retailer, the more formalized the training. Whether you enter the field via store management or buying depends primarily on the employer. Many stores separate these functions beginning at the entry level. You must choose which path you prefer. Other stores will introduce all new merchandising personnel to buying and later allow those interested in and qualified for management to move up. The opposite arrangement, moving into buying at some later stage, also occurs, although infrequently.

The modern store is reaping the benefits of the technological revolution. Point-of-sale computer terminals are replacing mechanical cash registers. These automatically compute sales, taxes, and discounts and simplify inventory control by keeping sales records. Computers are also used for credit records and tracking sales forecasts.

Retailing is vulnerable to downturns in the economy, but it's one of the first industries to bounce back after a recession. As a highly profit-oriented business, it's hectic and competitive. The customer's satisfaction and loyalty to the store are very important, which means that you must tolerate and even pamper people whom you may not like. In retailing, the unexpected is the order of the day. You can expect to feel pressured, but seldom unchallenged.

JOB OUTLOOK

JOB OPENINGS WILL GROW: As fast as average

COMPETITION FOR JOBS: Keen

In merchandising, the most competition exists in buying; this area has fewer openings, tends to pay a bit better and has an aura of glamour about it.

NEW JOB OPPORTUNITIES: Most department store chains have re-
trenched over the past few years. The days when department stores
sold everything from appliances to zippers are pretty much gone.
Most chains now focus their attention on items that provide them
with the highest markup (price above cost) and lowest inventory
costs. Clothing, of course, is the merchandise line most vital to the
retail department store business. Clothing buyers have become
probably the most important employees in the retail business. With
increased competition from smaller boutiques, larger stores need
merchandise that will keep customers coming back. It's up to buyers
to get that merchandise into the stores.

GEOGRAPHIC JOB INDEX

The location of retail jobs parallels the distribution of the general
population; stores operate where customers live. As an up-and-
coming executive in a retail chain, expect to work in a city or
suburban area. Most new store construction in the coming years is
expected to take place in revitalizing city cores. Department stores
are found across the country, with the highest concentration of jobs
in the Northeast, Midwest and West Coast.

If your interest is buying, your geographic options are more
limited. For many department store chains, most or all buying takes
place in a few key markets, notably New York, NY.

WHO THE EMPLOYERS ARE

A retailer is, in its simplest definition, a third party who sells a
producer's goods to a consumer for a profit. The retailing industry
as a whole comprises a wide variety of stores of different sizes with
different personnel needs. Management personnel are sought by all
major retail firms, including grocery, drug, specialty, and variety
store chains, but because the most varied opportunities are found in
department stores, this chapter focuses on this sector of retailing.

MAJOR EMPLOYERS

Federated Department Stores and Allied Stores Corporation, Cincinnati, OH

Abraham & Straus
Bloomingdale's
Bon Marché
Lazarus
Stern's
Rich's

Carter Hawley Hale Stores, Los Angeles, CA

The Broadway
Emporium Capwell
Weinstock's

Dayton Hudson Corporation, Minneapolis, MN

Dayton's
Hudson Stores
Leachmere
Mirvin's
Target Stores

R.H. Macy & Company, New York, NY

Marshall Fields, Chicago, IL
Montgomery Ward & Company, Chicago, IL
J.C. Penney Company, New York, NY
Sears, Roebuck & Company, Chicago, IL

HOW TO BREAK INTO THE FIELD

Your best bet is on-campus interviews. Major retailers actively recruit on college campuses. This is the most accessbile way to most potential employers. Don't hesistate, however, to contact employers directly, especially if you want to work for a smaller operation. Read the business section of your newspaper regularly to find out about store expansions, the addition of new stores, or locations and other developments in retailing that can provide important clues to new job openings. Keep in mind that retail or selling experience of any kind will increase your chances of getting hired.

INTERNATIONAL JOB OPPORTUNITIES

Extremely limited. Opportunities to live abroad exist at the corporate level of a few international chains.

DEPARTMENT STORE RETAILING ENTREPRENEUR

Chocolate chip cookies next to the fine china? Candy across from the cable-knit sweaters?

Department stores are always looking for products and attractions that entice customers inside their doors. To get those attractions while keeping costs at a minimum, some chains have entered into arrangements with small, independent retailers that specialize in particular products. Essentially, these small retailers lease space inside department stores to sell their wares.

One such entrepreneurial success story is David's Cookies. David's got its start in the 1970s in New York City. Originally a one-storefront operation, David's quickly became a ubiquitous part of the Manhattan street scene, as cookie-hungry patrons discovered the wonders of macadamia-nut chocolate chips, white chocolate chips, and other such tempting morsels.

As David's Cookies grew, its appeal to upscale shoppers wasn't lost on department store moguls. The fit was ideal. Department stores needed high-quality, high-profile offerings to increase patronage, and David's needed an outlet for expansion. So it was that David's entered into a working agreement with the R.H. Macy department store chain, and with its blue-and-white logo set up shop right inside Macy's stores.

STORE MANAGEMENT

If you're a "people person," consider the store management side of merchandising. You'll be responsible for handling the needs of staff and customers.

The job of store management personnel, even at entry level, entails making decisions on your own. But since decisions often have to be made on the spot and involve balancing the interests of both customers and the store, your mistakes are likely to be highly visible. Whether you manage the smallest department or a very large store, you must always keep the bottom line—making a profit—in mind when making decisions.

During training, you will work with experienced managers and will be moved throughout the store to observe all aspects of merchandising. If you're quick to learn and demonstrate management potential, you'll soon be made manager of a small department or assistant manager of a large one. You will have a fair amount of autonomy, but you must stick to store standards and implement policies determined by higher level management.

QUALIFICATIONS

PERSONAL: Ability to learn quickly. Enormous enthusiasm. The flexibility to handle a constantly changing schedule. Willingness to work weekends, holidays, and nights.

PROFESSIONAL: Demonstrated leadership ability. Ability to work with figures, finances, inventories, and quotas. A sense of diplomacy.

CAREER PATHS

LEVEL	JOB TITLE	EXPERIENCE NEEDED
Entry	Department manager trainee	College degree
2	Group department manager	2–3 years
3	Assistant store manager	5–10 years
4	Store manager	8–12 years

JOB RESPONSIBILITIES ♦ ENTRY LEVEL

THE BASICS: Handling staff scheduling. Dealing with customer complaints. Doing plenty of paperwork.

MORE CHALLENGING DUTIES: Monitoring and motivating your sales staff. Assisting in the selection of merchandise for your department. Making decisions and solving problems.

MOVING UP

Advancement in store management depends on how well you shoulder responsibility and take advantage of opportunities to learn. Effectively leading your staff, moving merchandise, and, above all, turning a profit, will secure your promotion into higher levels.

Your first management position will be overseeing a small department, handling greater volumes of money and merchandise. The group department manager directs several department managers, coordinating store operations on a larger scale. From here you might progess to assistant store manager and store manager. This last position is, in many respects, similar to running a private business. The best may then go on to the corporate level.

PROMOTIONS

Relocations is often necessary in order to win promotions. Switching store locations every three years or so is not uncommon. However, depending on the chain, a change of workplace need not require a change of address; often stores are within easy driving distance of each other. But the larger the chain, the greater the possibility that you'll have to move to a different city to further your career.

BUYING

Do you fantasize about a shopping spree in the world's fashion capitals? A few lucky buyers, after years of work and experience, are paid to do just that when they're sent to Hong Kong, Paris, or Milan to select new lines of merchandise. Most do not make it to such heights, but on a smaller scale, this is the business of buying.

A buyer decides which goods will be available in a store. Buyers authorize merchandise purchases from wholesalers and set the retail prices. A sensitivity to changing trends, tastes, and styles and an ability to understand and forecast the preference of your own store's customers are crucial. Buyers must also maintain standards of quality while keeping within certain ranges of affordability.

The buyer who works for a discount department store faces a particularly tough job. Obtaining lower-than-average prices for quality merchandise is a real challenge and requires an unerring eye and an ability to negotiate with sellers.

Astute buying translates into profits for the store and advancement for your career. Learning how to spend large sums of money wisely takes practice. Fortunately, as a new buyer you can afford to make a few mistakes, even an occasional expensive one, without jeopardizing your career. A good buyer takes calculated risks, and as you gain experience more of your choices will succeed.

During training, you'll work immediately as an assistant to an experienced buyer. The trainee progresses by observing, asking questions, and offering to take on appropriate responsibilities.

QUALIFICATIONS

PERSONAL: An interest in changing trends and fashions. An ability to work with a wide variety of personalities. A willingness to channel creativity into a commercial enterprise.

PROFESSIONAL: Financial and negotiating know-how. Organizational skills. Good judgment in spotting trends and evaluating products.

CAREER PATHS

LEVEL	JOB TITLE	EXPERIENCE NEEDED
Entry	Assistant or junior buyer	College degree and store training
2	Buyer (small lines)	2–5 years
3	Buyer (large lines)	4–10 years
4	Corporate merchandise manager	15+ years

JOB RESPONSIBILITIES ♦ ENTRY LEVEL

THE BASICS: Assisting your supervising buyer. Placing orders and speaking with manufacturers by phone. Supervising the inspection and unpacking of new merchandise and overseeing its distribution.

MORE CHALLENGING DUTIES: Becoming acquainted with various manufacturers' lines. Considering products for purchase. Evaluating your store's needs. Keeping an eye on the competition.

MOVING UP

Advancement depends on proof of your ability to judge customer needs and to choose saleable goods. The only purchases closely scrutinized by higher authorities are those inconsistent with past practices and standards.

After completing your training, you will first buy for a small department, then, as you become seasoned, for larger departments. High-placed buyers make decisions in buying for a key department common to several stores, for an entire state, or possibly for many stores. Your buying plans must always be well coordinated with the needs of store management.

FASHION COORDINATION

The job of fashion coordinator exists only in some large department stores. The coordinator takes over part of the role held by buyers in most stores by offering advice to the buying staff on changing tastes, trends, and styles. Where fashion coordinators are employed, they work with the buying staff to ensure that the store's merchandise is completely up-to-date. Although fashion coordination staffs tend to be small, this specialized area allows art majors to exercise their visual talents in an exciting way.

In most cases, fashion coordination is not a career path job in the traditional sense. Although recent graduates may find entry-level jobs as assistants, more often retail personnel move into fashion coordination from merchandising or other areas. To vie for this exciting position you must be able to demonstrate your talents through an exceptional portfolio, which should include examples of fashion design. However, fashion coordinators are not the "artsy" people of the retail industry. Their decisions must be grounded in a solid business sense and an understanding of customer needs.

As in buying, travel can be an important part of the job, especially in a department that sells imported goods. Domestic manufacturers will usually send their own representatives to introduce product lines, but overseas producers expect American retailers to come to them. In some cases, this can mean up to five months a year spent in Asia or Europe. You will probably work harder on your travels than when you are in the store, but you will be treated royally by producers anxious to make a sale.

Because this is such a small area, personal contacts with decision makers in the industry and a proven reputation in the retail business are essential to landing such a position.

DISPLAY

Like fashion coordinating, display is a specialized area employing talented people with art backgrounds. Each season brings the need for new merchandise presentations that must grab the eye of the shopper or passerby. Display people design and implement the window decorations and interior displays that are so important in promoting sales.

Smaller stores will often handle their display needs through outside agencies or free lancers, but career opportunities exist with many large retailers. Display is a small field with low turnover, so openings are quite limited.

As in all retail positions, the recent graduate begins as an apprentice or assistant, and professional skills are learned entirely on the job. Display efforts are coordinated with store management. The department managers are ultimately responsible for the appearance of their sales floors and know the merchandise well, so their input is crucial.

Good display requires more than creativity and originality. Its greatest challenge is working within limitations of time, space, and money. Although more removed from business concerns than other areas of retailing, display personnel must have an appreciation of changing styles—both in the look of merchandise and in the way it is presented to the public.

ADDITIONAL INFORMATION

SALARIES

Entry-level salaries range from $16,000 to $25,000 a year, depending on the employer and the geographic location of the store. Junior buyers tend to be among the best paid entry-level employees.

The following salary ranges show typical annual salaries for experienced retail personnel. In merchandising and fashion coordination, salaries vary with the size and importance of your department.

2–4 years:	$20,000–30,000
5–10 years:	$30,000–45,000
12 years or more:	$40,000 and up

WORKING CONDITIONS

HOURS: Most retail personnel work a five-day, 40-hour week, but schedules vary with different positions. In store management, daily shifts are rarely nine to five, because stores are open as many as 12 hours a day, seven days a week. Night, weekend, and holiday duty are unavoidable, especially for newcomers. Operations personnel work similar hours. Buyers, fashion coordinators, and display people have more regular schedules and are rarely asked to work evening and weekend hours.

ENVIRONMENT: In merchandising, your time is divided between the office and the sales floor, more often the latter. Office space at the entry level may or may not be private, depending on the store. Whether you share space or not, expect to be close to the sales floor. Merchandising is no place for those who need absolute privacy and quiet in order to be productive.

Expect to find yourself in similar surroundings in fashion coordination and display.

WORKSTYLE: In store management, office time is 100 percent work. Every valuable moment must be used effectively to keep on top of the paperwork. On the floor you will be busy overseeing the arrangement of merchandise, meeting with your sales staff, and listening to customer complaints. Long hours on your feet will test your patience and endurance, but you can never let the weariness show. In buying and fashion coordination, office time is spent with paperwork and calls to manufacturers. You might also review catalog copy and illustrations. On the sales floor, you'll meet with store personnel to see how merchandise is displayed and, most important, to see how the customers are responding. Manufacturers' representatives will visit to show their products, and you might spend some days at manufacturer and wholesaler showrooms. Because these jobs bring you into the public eye, you must be well dressed and meticulously groomed. The generous discounts that employees receive as a fringe benefit help defray the cost of maintaining a wardrobe.

Display personnel spend time meeting with management personnel to formulate display plans. You will set up in-store displays during times of light business, so you won't interfere with shoppers.

TRAVEL: In most job areas, your responsibility lies with your own department and your own store; travel opportunities are virtually nonexistent, except for some top-level personnel. Buyers and fashion coordinators are exceptions. Here you may make annual trips to New York, NY, and other key cities. You might also travel to trade shows in which your type of merchandise is displayed.

EXTRACURRICULAR ACTIVITIES/WORK EXPERIENCE

Leadership in campus organizations
Treasurer or financial officer of an organization
Sales position on the yearbook or campus newspaper
Summer or part-time work in any aspect of retailing

INTERNSHIPS

Arrange internships with individual stores or chains; many are eager to hire interns, preferring students who are in the fall semester of their senior year. Check with your school's placement or internship office or with the store itself in the spring for a fall internship. Summer internships are also available with some stores. Contact the placement office or the personnel departments of individual stores for details.

RECOMMENDED READING

BOOKS
Opportunities in Retailing Careers, by Roslyn Dolber, NTC Publishing Group: 1989

Contemporary Retailing, Third Ed., by William H. Bolen, Prentice-Hall: 1988

Directory of Department Stores and Mail Order Firms, by the editors of Chain Store Guide, Lebhar Friedman Inc.: revised periodically

Macy's for Sale, by Isadore Barmash, Weidenfeld & Nicolson: 1989

Retail Management: A Strategic Approach, Fourth Ed., by Barry Berman and Joel R. Evans, McGraw-Hill: 1989

PERIODICALS

Advertising Age (weekly), Crain Communications, 740 North Rush Street, Chicago, IL 60611

Journal of Retailing (quarterly), New York University, Stern School of Business, 40 West 4th Street, Rm. 202, New York, NY 10003

Stores (monthly), National Retail Merchants Association, 100 West 31st Street, New York, NY 10001

Women's Wear Daily (daily), Fairchild Publications, Inc., 7 East 12th Street, New York, NY 10003

PROFESSIONAL ASSOCIATIONS

American Retail Federation
1616 H Street, N.W.
Washington, DC 20006

National Retail Merchants Association
100 West 31st Street
New York, NY 10001

INTERVIEWS

FASHION COORDINATOR
MAJOR DEPARTMENT STORE
NEW YORK, NY

My first job was far removed from retailing—I taught high school math for a year. The school environment really didn't excite me and I felt I could get more from a job. I saw an ad for the position of fashion coordinator at a branch of Gimbels' department store. I wasn't planning a career in retailing, but because I kept up with fashion and felt I had a flair for it, I applied. I got the job and enjoyed the work, but that particular branch was not a high-caliber store, and after two years I was ready to move on.

I took a part-time job as an assistant manager at an Ann Taylor store, one of a chain selling women's clothing. At that time I was also going to school to finish an art degree. My job included store management and some limited buying. I wound up managing my own store, but because Ann Taylor has a small management staff, I felt there wasn't enough growth potential. I came to know the man who was doing store design for the chain. He was expanding his operations and needed help, so I went to work with him. I designed store interiors and fixtures, which gave me a whole new perspective on the industry. I have been lucky to see so many sides of retailing, but these job changes also required me to relocate.

When I moved into fashion coordination with my present employer about seven years ago, I finally found what I had been looking for—a high-powered, high-pressured environment. When I walk into the store each morning I feel that things are moving, happening. That's the fun of retailing.

My responsibility is to work with the buyers, helping them choose the right styles. After you've been in retailing a number of years, you know where fashion has been and you can see where it's going. You decide, really by making educated guesses, what the public will want a year from today. My job includes a lot of travel—

usually eight or nine weeks a year. Where there are products abroad, we explore them. That's the only way to keep up with the competition.

In buying we speak of hundreds of dozens, so you must be volume-oriented. You ask, "What does our regular customer want to see?" Then you make a decision that has to be more right than wrong. I work with children's wear, a department that rarely sees radical changes in style. But there are always new trends in color and design, and new products.

One of the toughest parts of my job is training new buyers and helping with their first big buys. They are understandably nervous about spending several hundred thousand dollars. The fashion coordinator is one with buying experience. You offer better advice if you understand the pressure and monetary responsibility of the buyer's job.

Even though I'm in a creative area, business and financial concerns are of the highest importance. You must have a head for business in every retailing job. You want to find beautiful quality products, but if they don't sell, you've failed.

The one drawback to my job is advancement. My talents and experience are best used right where I am now. Unlike the buyers, I really have no place higher to go. But I enjoy my work. I suppose it's like being an artist, and how many artists are really appreciated?

SUSAN HARRINGTON
BLOOMINGDALE'S DEPARTMENT STORE
NEWTON, MA

I was a flight attendant my first two years out of college. The company went bankrupt. I had an opportunity to go to a larger airline carrier, but I decided I didn't want to be a flight attendant for the rest of my life. It's easier to make a career change in your early twenties than 10 or 15 years later. I took a job selling cosmetics over the counter at a department store. They told me that even though I had a four year degree, everyone starts on the counter. After about eight months I felt discouraged. I had been the top salesperson consistently, but there was no promotion on the horizon. Looking back at it now, with a little more professional maturity, I can see that, although every company likes to promote on the basis of merit, if there is no opening or a job they can't always create one for you. I think retail is like advertising and a lot of other occupations that sound glamourous. The pyramid narrows dramatically once you get beyond the entry level. There's a lot of people who want top positions who are qualified for them.

I worked in a retail position in a department store that also had a lot of vendor support with the idea that I could either grow with the store or with the vendor. This didn't happen so I worked at MCI in telemarketing sales and strangely enough, the woman who had been my counter manager for the cosmetics vendor was recruited by another cosmetics company. She hired me to work on her special sales team for a year-and-a-half. I then went to being a personnel consultant for a personnel agency for a year and a half. I wasn't interested in this as a career, but I needed it on my résumé. And from there I got this job because of my retail experience.

Unless you are one of the few who get a position in a management trainee program out of college—and these positions are very limited because we only recruit from a certain list of schools—you take a sales position. My employer offers a lucrative opportunity because our people work on straight commission. While you are waiting to get your foot in the door at least you can make some money. Your initiative and your productivity determines your salary. We feel that these jobs are appropriate for people with a four year degree. Unfortunately most people with a four year degree are not realistic about their position and salary potential. The track here is to go from being a salesperson to being a DMT (Department Manager in Training) to being a Department Manager to being a Divisional, who oversees department managers, and from there being a store manager. This is your local option. All the buying opportunities are out of New York.

People move up this career path based on their merits. We look for people who are realistic, dedicated, and pay attention to detail. We are interested in people who are providing exceptional customer service. We want people to treat this job like a professional sales opportunity. People who treat their customers like special clients, call them on the phone, write them notes, let them know about special events, and invite them in to shop by appointment. If you are interested in department store retailing, there is a lot of opportunity, and something like the commission system at our store can increase your earning potential tremendously.

TOM WENSINGER
COORDINATOR OF EXECUTIVE RECRUITMENT
NEIMAN-MARCUS
DALLAS, TX

I was recruited from campus. I graduated from Texas A & M about four years ago and I went right into the executive development program here at Neiman-Marcus. Recently I took this job where I do the recruitment for that program. Before, I was an assistant buyer in the Men's Division and an assistant buyer in the Ladies Shoe Division.

Our merchandise divisions are centralized, so we do all of our purchasing out of Dallas for stores across the country. Now that doesn't mean that we buy all of our merchandise here in Dallas, but the offices are here and all these activities are coordinated from here. A lot of the assistant buyer's job is communication with department managers across the country, relaying strategies about merchandise flow. All of the day-to-day activities that require input from the buying office more often than not go through the assistant buyer. Also, the assistant buyer's job is very much apprentice oriented in that by the time you accomplish your role as assistant buyer you should be a buyer. That is the goal of being an assistant buyer.

As a coordinator of executive recruitment I am responsible for the hiring and placement of all people within the executive development program. Upon completion of this program I place them in their first job as an assistant buyer. Just like buying goes beyond buying, recruiting goes beyond recruiting. More often than not you do a lot of support work in department store retailing. For instance, you have to have a marketing orientation as an assistant buyer. You are a product manager. For all this merchandise that your buyer is buying, you have to do a lot of analysis to see what is selling, what needs to be moved, what is not selling, what are the costs, what's the most effective way to distribute the merchandise.

Performance is the best way to move up in department store retailing. Advancement is dependent upon the company you work with and how they are willing to promote you. You have to get with a company that's willing to take a risk on you, and along with that risk they've got to give you an opportunity. Making people assistant buyers is risky, but the job has a lot of opportunity because the assistant buyer can exercise a lot of authority—more authority than you would get in a lot of jobs. Your authority develops individually. Somebody who comes right out of the training program won't have a lot of authority. They develop that after a couple of years on the job. Your authority grows as you develop to make buys. Your buyer works with you and lets you select the merchandise. You have the authority to transfer merchandise and make cost-related decisions between stores. You negotiate with vendors. There's also a lot of clerical and office work.

I'd want a job applicant to be bright. I'd want them to demonstrate a history of success in whatever they had done. I don't think they would have to necessarily have worked in a retail store to be interesting to us. I would just want them to have done well in whatever they did, be it academics, extracurricular activities, leadership, athletics, or work experience. I want them to have valuable work experience. That doesn't mean that busing tables is less valuable than working in a store or doing an internship. A lot of times you learn a lot more busing tables.

For college graduates, I would encourage them to find a training program within the company as opposed to working on the sales floor and working themselves up. The best way to do this is make an appointment with a campus recruiter. If your college doesn't have any recruitment, then you'll have to send out résumés and try to get to see a recruiter. You would be most successful in gaining an interview in the area of the company's headquarters.

Now, don't get me wrong about the value of being on the floor. After you are an assistant buyer at Neiman-Marcus you are promoted to department manager. I think that being out there on the floor as a department manager for two years is completely necessary. But for someone who wants to be a retail executive, a corporate training program will provide the floor experience without building in that extra rung of sales. If you do start in sales, you would work through their individual store management. You get a department manager's position and then you get nominated for the training program. And then we bring them to Dallas and we put them on the buying career path.

My general advice is that this is a fast paced environment, but if you don't love it, don't do it. I find that if you don't love retailing, you'll hate it.

FASHION, TEXTILE, AND INTERIOR DESIGN

From the first pair of trousers worn in sixth century B.C. Persia to the pair of sneakers you wear to your aerobics class, clothing looks and feels good because of the creativity and technical skills of a designer. A designer, whether for apparel, accessories, interiors, or textiles, is an applied artist concerned with the function and appearance of articles we use everyday, as well as with the places in which we live and work. Good designs not only work, but please the eye, provide pleasant surroundings and promote good spirits.

The word fashion exudes a glamorous and exciting image of runway shows, beautiful clothes, and Paris couture houses. The industry encompasses much more than that. Unlike other industries such as automobiles or computers, the fashion industry is not limited to a single product or type of product. Besides apparel production, it includes accessories, fibers, fabrics, interiors, and home furnishings.

The only element that remains constant in the fashion business is change. Because styles and preferences evolve continually, people in the field need to be open to and aware of new ideas and influences. The creativity demanded by the business does not happen in a vacuum but is fed by current events, art, science, nature, ideas, and people. Creative work can be exciting because it must keep one step ahead of consumer tastes; fulfilling when your ideas are adopted and appreciated by many.

At the same time, however, creative work can be frustrating during periods when new ideas don't come easily or when a customer's preferences clash with those of the designer. Even the world's most famous fashion designers can be left stung, and in some cases embarrassed, when what seemed like brilliant ideas to them fall flat with their customers. In the late 1980s, for instance, the leading design houses almost unanimously touted the miniskirt as *the* fashion trend. Almost unanimously, women—particularly in America—disagreed. The result: The miniskirt revolution was stopped dead in its tracks. Fashion design is a business, after all, and the bottom line is meeting the consumer's needs and tastes.

Those employed in the apparel industry tend to change jobs frequently. Because so much of the business is seasonal, particularly in apparel design, and because public tastes change rapidly, there is a constant demand for new talent. This, along with the variety of articles and services produced by the fashion industry, creates career opportunities for those with new and interesting ideas, good skills, and stamina for long hours and a fast pace.

The fashion industry incorporates many disciplines, so it is especially important that graduates entering the field have some educational concentrations in specific areas: apparel design, fine arts, textile design, pattern making, or interior design. A portfolio is essential and must reflect talent in that particular concentration in a variety of ways. Specifically, skills in manual dexterity, sketching, and garment construction are essential to the apparel designer; strong two-dimensional artistic rendering ability and excellent color sense to the textile designer; and an understanding of three-dimensional space efficiency, furnishings, fabrics, and color coordination to the interior designer.

New technology and training is affecting the industry from all angles. Computers, for instance, are beginning to be used in a number of areas: printing, weaving and knitting of textiles; apparel inventory, color coordination and forecasting; space relationships; and drafting techniques. Familiarity with computers and the ability to analyze data is increasingly beneficial to those entering the business, designers included!

JOB OUTLOOK

JOB OPENINGS WILL GROW: As fast as average.

COMPETITION FOR JOBS: Keen

NEW JOB OPPORTUNITIES: The apparel industry will continue to expand its scope as long as there are new ideas, new technology, new influences on fashion. For instance, in the last few years the surge of interest in fitness and health has brought with it new lines of apparel to accommodate running, aerobics, and dancing enthusiasts. Dressing has become less standardized and more individualized and this has led to greater diversity in the apparel that the industry produces.

Although there continue to be new developments and innovation in textile technology—witness the Lycra explosion of the late 1980s—there has also been a significant shift to overseas imports, causing the domestic cloth-producing industry to bog down. Although textile designers are still in demand, the job market for these professionals has definitely tightened in the past decade, and the prospects for a reversal of that trend are not promising.

For the interior designer, opportunities have broadened in the last few years to include everything from airplanes to banks to living rooms. The interior designer used to be called a decorator, but decorating is only one aspect of the designer's many responsibilities now. Also, more people are living in smaller spaces, which has created a greater demand for the interior designer to be an engineer of efficiency as well as of beauty and personality in living environments.

GEOGRAPHIC JOB INDEX

At least two-thirds of the textile and apparel manufacturers are concentrated on the East Coast, with textile mills in the southern states and apparel firms centered in the New York, NY, metropolitan area. Textile designers will find the largest concentration of job opportunities in the New York, NY, area, however, as many of the mills base their design operations in the city. Smaller, more specialized textile design firms may also be found in other large cities where apparel is produced. The apparel industry is no longer limited to New York, NY. Although a large share of the market operates there, an increasing volume pours out of California, along with other areas such as Texas, the New England region, and Chicago, IL. Various cities or regions may specialize in different types of apparel, so if you're pursuing a particular area of design, you may want to situate yourself in the region that produces that type of apparel in volume. For instance, ski and outerwear comes out of New England, Seattle, WA, and Denver, CO, among other places; swimwear out of California; men's suits out of Chicago, IL.

Large commercial buildings enterprises may seek out top interior design firms located in New York, NY or other big cities. Generally, however, a company, whether it is small or a Fortune 500 company, will select a designer or firm from its own city, particularly for convenience, as the designer must be on site and with the client to supervise every detail of an interior project. Well-known interior designers may be imported or called in for consultation, especially if they are known for a certain look or aspect of design such as hotel lobbies. The demand for quality environmental design exists in virtually every region, so interior design and architectural firms will be found nationwide.

WHO THE EMPLOYERS ARE

APPAREL MANUFACTURERS produce a large volume of apparel merchandise that is sold to a mass market, specifically in lower price ranges.

DESIGNER LICENSEES are divisions that produce apparel and accessories under a specific designer label.

PATTERN COMPANIES print patterns and instructions for the home sewer. They also provide fabric tips, fashion forecasts, educational workshops and monthly publications.

TEXTILE MILLS turn raw materials into cloth in a variety of ways including weaving, knitting, tufting, and nonwoven methods, to be used in everything from apparel to home furnishings to tires. The process may be performed from beginning to finished product in a single vertical operation or may utilize converters, changing hands in midpoint.

TEXTILE DESIGN STUDIOS function as service operations to textile mills and converters, providing designs, colorings, and repeats (repetition of a single design element to create a total design) to individual clients.

COMMERCIAL DESIGN FIRMS deal with standardized contract designing of commercial interiors such as banks, offices, stores, and other public places.

RESIDENTIAL DESIGN FIRMS deal with interiors of homes or particular rooms in a house.

INTERIOR DESIGN DEPARTMENTS may function as an individually managed department within a retail store or as a division of a hotel or restaurant chain.

FREE LANCE OPPORTUNITIES are available in apparel, textile and interior design to those with special skills and self-motivation. Although for your first job in the industry it is advisable to work under experienced professionals in an established company, a free lance career can be a satisfying and rewarding lifestyle after you gain some marketable skills and experience.

MAJOR EMPLOYERS

Below is a sampling of employers involved in the various aspects of design.

APPAREL

Blue Bell, Greensboro, NC
Cheesebrough-Pond's, Inc., Greenwich, CT
Hart, Marx Corp., Chicago, IL
Jonathon Logan, New York, NY
Manhattan Industries, New York, NY
Oxford Industries, Atlanta, GA
Palm Beach Inc., Cincinnati, OH
Russ Togs, New York, NY
Levi Strauss, San Francisco, CA
U.S. Industries, Inc., Stamford, CT
V. P. Corporation, Wyomissing, PA

HOME SEWING

Butterick Co. Inc., New York, NY
McCall Pattern Company, New York, NY
Simplicity Pattern Company, New York, NY

TEXTILE MILLS AND CONVERTERS

Burlington, Greensboro, NC
Collins and Aikman, New York, NY
Dan River, Danville, VA
E. I. DuPont de Nemours & Co., Wilmington, DE
Fieldcrest Mills, Inc., Eden, NC
Hoechst Celanese Corp., New York, NY
Springs Industries, Fort Mill, SC
J. P. Stevens, New York, NY
West Point-Pepperell, West Point, GA

INTERIOR DESIGN

Consult the director of the American Society of Interior Designers for designer firms in specific areas. Unlike in other areas, the top, well-known designer firms are usually small, offering only a few entry-level opportunities.

HOW TO BREAK INTO THE FIELD

Your portfolio is your ticket into the fashion arena, so you should spend considerable time and effort preparing and perfecting it. Ask professors and professionals to critique it and make suggestions for improvement before you show it to a potential employer. Include a variety of art media and subject matter, even if you're specializing in a particular area of design. Try to include some professional projects you may have completed as an intern or apprentice, besides your class assignments. Interior designer applicants should include a set of working/construction drawings, either from schoolwork or from a firm you've worked for. The fashion industry is one that demands talent and fresh ideas. Your portfolio should be an expression of the creative energy you can provide to an employer.

School placement offices—especially if you have attended a fashion school—are particularly helpful, not only because they understand the industry but because the industry trusts and uses them. The larger apparel-producing cities will have employment agencies that specialize in fashion and art positions.

The help-wanted section of your daily newspaper will list opportunities under fashion, apparel, design, textiles, home furnishings, or interiors. Write a professional yet creative letter that you can vary according to each particular ad. After consulting industry directories, write a letter to accompany your résumé and send it cold to top firms in your discipline. Many of them will respond with brochures or information about their companies that will orient you to their specific needs. Especially helpful are the trade newspapers such as *Women's Wear Daily*, the *Daily News Record*, and *Home Furnishings Daily*, which usually list job opportunities in their classified sections.

Spend some time with professionals, not with the intention of getting a job through them, but to interview them about *their* work. It may lead to valuable industry contacts and information. Internships and apprenticeships can provide excellent contacts as well, and might eventually lead to jobs.

A number of professionals and labor organizations reflect various interests in the fashion industry. Some provide career information, resources, publications, lectures, and workshops for students.

INTERNATIONAL JOB OPPORTUNITIES

Because of high unemployment rates in many other countries, the likelihood of getting a job overseas—especially in a glamorous field such as fashion—is very slim unless one possesses unique design skills. With many manufacturers importing labor and materials from overseas, bilingual skills, particularly in Asian languages, can be most valuable to employers here in facilitating efficient communications with foreign counterparts.

FASHION, TEXTILE, AND INTERIOR DESIGN ENTREPRENEUR

The design business is entrepreneurial by nature. When you think of fashion designers, for instance, people, not corporate entities, come to mind: Ralph Lauren, Christian Dior, Perry Ellis, Yves Saint Laurent, and so on. Never mind that successful designers like these usually do become corporate entities; without that initial creative and individual spark, their names would never have become known.

Ironically, however, setting up an entrepreneurial career may be more difficult in the design business than in any other endeavor short of manufacturing automobiles or heavy equipment. That's because name recognition is everything; an unknown designer has little chance for success, be it in fashion, textile, or interior design.

For this reason, most independent designers spend years making reputations for themselves inside established design studios and houses. Although a creation by Jane Smith for, say, Calvin Klein will bear Calvin's name and not Jane's, insiders will certainly learn who Jane Smith is if her work is good enough to merit attention. Building reputations inside the design establishment has enabled many creative individuals to embark on careers as independent designers.

APPAREL DESIGN

The largest number of apparel designers are employed by manufacturers who mass-produce clothing in the lower price range. These volume houses rarely originate fashion but tend to be followers, adapting styles to meet the price requirements of their customers. There may be many designers in these firms, each designing for a different division. In larger apparel firms, a designer may have one or more assistant designers; in smaller firms, the designer may work alone.

The workstyle in the design room will vary. In smaller firms such as name designer licensees, a designer may work independently, meeting periodically with the name designer for consultation and supervision. Pattern company design rooms tend to be team-oriented, incorporating the input of designer, pattern-maker, and instruction-writer.

A designer can't come up with creative ideas if he or she is cooped up day after day in the design room. You must shop the stores for ideas; research historical and contemporary trends in the libraries, museums, and galleries; be aware of current events; and peruse fashion and other periodicals frequently.

You must, in many cases, also supervise and plan work for assistants, become involved with salespeople and clients to get a feel for what sells, work closely with stylists to determine the look and colors for that particular season, and have good rapport with production workers and management.

Generally a designer is expected to create a line for four seasons per year. Quite often in women's wear, a company will have five or six lines, including separate groups for holiday and resort wear. With 40 to 75 items in a typical line, you must be able to meet deadlines, deal with pressure, manage time, think conceptually, and keep creativity flowing.

QUALIFICATIONS

PERSONAL: Natural creativity. A capacity to handle pressure, deadlines, and long hours. An ability to make decisions. Self-motivation and initiative.

PROFESSIONAL: Artistic ability, including two- and three-dimensional aptitude. A flair for color and clothing coordination. An eye for trends. Team spirit. Problem-solving and technical aptitude. Working knowledge of clothing construction.

CAREER PATHS

LEVEL	JOB TITLE	EXPERIENCE NEEDED
Entry	Assistant designer, cutting assistant	College or fashion school degree
2	Assistant technical designer	1–2 years
3	Pattern company designer, designer	3–5 years
4	Head designer	10+ years

JOB RESPONSIBILITIES ♦ ENTRY LEVEL

THE BASICS: Clerical duties. Preparation of presentations or boards—fabric renderings and apparel sketches. Shopping the markets for styles, fabrics, trims.

MORE CHALLENGING DUTIES: Consulting with designer about new design ideas. Offering original ideas. Making first patterns—draping with muslin or drafting on paper.

MOVING UP

If you demonstrate ability to follow through with ideas, to make wise shopping choices in the markets, and to understand the various components of creating a line, your promotion to designer should be forthcoming. How fast it comes will depend on the structure of the company. As a designer you will be responsible for creating your own lines. This requires a flair for coordinating a number of different pieces of clothing and colors into a harmonious whole. You will work with the stylist and the merchandising staff to develop a theme or statement that your designs will reflect.

In some firms where there is a well-known, established head designer, you may become an assistant technical designer. Rather than conceptualizing and executing your own designs, you will work closely with the designer.

As a designer you will work directly with clients. This may involve some travel. You might also interact with textile mills, overseas manufacturers, and suppliers. As you grow with the company and gain more responsibility in the operational capacity, you may actually design less and less. If you choose to, you can move into a business and merchandising position, giving overall direction to what goes into each line, setting prices, supervising production, and working directly with buyers. From there you would progress to marketing management.

If you elect, however, to continue as a designer, you will want to work for firms that will offer you increasing design responsibility and fewer restrictions so that you become established either as a house designer or, eventually, as an independent name designer.

TEXTILE DESIGN

Widely diverse talents are required because the textile industry is an art and a science as well as a business. Artistic, creative, managerial, scientific, and technical skills are necessary for an efficient and productive industry.

In the United States, approximately one million people are employed in the business of turning raw materials into cloth and bringing the finished product to the consumer. Each segment of the industry, generally, is centered in a different part of the country.

Most of the design work in textile companies is handled in New York, NY, as the major textile firms tend to base their design and styling departments there.

Different types of operations, weaving, knitting, tufting and nonwoven mills, produce different types of textiles. Some textile companies operate in more than one of these categories and diversify further into such areas as chemicals, plastics, and rubber products. Some concentrate entirely on one category. Manufacturing companies are organized in one of two ways: a vertical operation, which incorporates all phases of the production process from fiber to finished fabric, or a greige mill, which produces greige goods—fabrics in an unfinished state. Converters are companies that finish the goods in a variety of ways.

The textile business has an effect on what people wear and on the fabrics they use in their homes and offices. Those who decide what yarns to use and what fabrics to create work six months to a year ahead of their counterparts in the garment industry. The merchandising and marketing staff, upon analyzing the market, gives direction to stylists who develop themes for lines and choose colors. The stylist then directs the staff of designers who create ideas and designs. The textile artist or colorist then takes the design and works it out on paper samples, experimenting with repeats and color combinations.

Those responsible for developing textile designs must function concurrently as artists, colorists, and technicians, as well as know all about fibers, styles, machinery, and fashion trends. All designers must have a good knowledge of fabric construction and production processes in addition to a strong sense of pattern and color.

To be most valuable to your employer, you won't lock yourself in your studio painting and drawing all day, but will work at broadening your range of skills and interests, becoming familiar with the latest changes in dyes, finishes, and equipment.

Jobs in textile design will be found in textile mills, textile converting houses, textile design studios, and vertical manufacturers. Most positions in the textile design area are full-time, but there are a number of free lance and short-term opportunities once you gain at least six months' experience and have the ambition to operate your own business.

QUALIFICATIONS

PERSONAL: Patience and persistence. Extreme neatness and accuracy. Imagination. Ability to follow instructions. Flexibility in dealing with other people.

PROFESSIONAL: Excellent artistic ability. Knowledge of fabric construction and production processes. Strong feeling for patterns and color. Understanding of machine capabilities. Forecasting sense.

CAREER PATHS

LEVEL	JOB TITLE	EXPERIENCE NEEDED
Entry	Colorist, repeat artist	Fashion or art school degree
2	Textile artist	2 years
3	Textile designer, assistant stylist	4–5 years
4	Stylist	7–10 years

JOB RESPONSIBILITIES ♦ ENTRY LEVEL

THE BASICS: Match and paint color combinations on designs or patterns created by the textile designer. Skillfully execute designs with paints or dyes. Research files or older fabrics for information about colors, dyes, and their effects on fabrics. Work out repeats.

MORE CHALLENGING DUTIES: Maintain swatch books and other records. Follow up on orders and deliveries. Set up appointments with customers. Maintain regular contact with mills to check on production processes. Troubleshoot for inventory, clerical details.

MOVING UP

As a designer you will be called on to execute original designs and to research fabric libraries, galleries, and museums for ideas and inspiration under the stylist's direction. You will develop specific ideas, coordinate designs, and begin to meet with clients. To move up, it is important to acquire technical knowledge of the capabilities and limitations of machinery used in production, and to know the cost production in order to design for specific price categories.

Your opportunity to continue moving up will depend on the structure of your firm's creative staff. Each textile firm will vary in size and diversity. After becoming well-established as a versatile textile designer and accruing considerable technical knowledge of production, you will either move up into a stylist or merchandising capacity or out of the mill structure and into a textile design business of your own. The stylist position incorporates many elements of the textile designer's responsibilities along with merchandising and sales and technical background. It is a demanding and diversified job that requires an extensive knowledge of the textile industry and a wide range of industry contacts and resources.

A key responsibility you will hold as a stylist will be to determine the look of a fabric line. You will provide direction to the textile designers and colorists as to what colors and types of patterns are to be used to create this look. If you are employed in a design studio, you may have a number of clients, each with different themes for their fabrics. At a large vertical textile manufacturer you may work on more than one line of fabrics each season to cater to different markets. Your organizational ability and conceptual thinking will be in great demand in operations of this nature and volume.

Frequent telephone contact with workers at the plant where fabric is printed, woven, or knitted will be part of your job as well as visits to the mill to check on strike-offs (samples of the fabric in production). It is essential that the production operation be closely supervised by your staff to assure color accuracy. Unless colors exactly match customer specifications, a lot of fabric and money will have been wasted. An alert stylist can prevent this.

In the sales capacity of your position, you will meet with customers to become familiar with their buying needs. It may also be part of your job to educate your clients in ways textiles can be used, and about treatment features and color coordination.

Large textile firms may hire several stylists and designers to cover responsibilities of different areas such as children's sleepwear, men's wool suitings, women's apparel, bed linens, and decorator fabrics and carpeting. Trade directories such as *Davison's Textile Bluebook* and *Davison's Textile Buyer's Guide*, published by Davison Publishing Inc., P.O. Box 477, Ridgewood, NJ 07451, will provide classification of types of products manufactured as well as geographic listings.

INTERIOR DESIGN

The business of designing and developing interiors incorporates two main areas: residential and commercial. In the residential area, steady clients are rare, because decorating a home does not require the same effort as decorating a bank office building. Also, homeowners do not redecorate often. Residential designing can provide a challenging and yet rewarding career as you solve design problems and create beautiful, efficient places for people to live.

Commercial firms operate on a contract basis and their clients include hotel chains, restaurants, banks, stores, office buildings, and hospitals—and even ship, auto, and aircraft manufacturers. Commercial interior design firms are offering an increasing number of services to their clients, becoming involved in real estate decisions and lease recommendations.

In recent years a great deal of research has been conducted on the way color and surroundings affect the psyche, improve or hinder work habits, encourage moods, create a high energy level, or provide a restful atmosphere, and increase or decrease the appetite. Corporations are looking to interior designers for more than merely pleasant surroundings for workers. An interior design consultant not only works with materials and space, but with personalities, tastes, life-styles, and business tactics.

Job progression and hands-on experience in designing interiors will vary according to the size of the firm. Firms with large-scale projects will use workers in specialized capacities; for instance, one person drafting, one designing, one choosing colors, one supervising the job site. Experience under top professionals will be valuable, but promotions may come about a bit more slowly. In firms of ten employees or fewer, you will take on greater responsibility faster and move into a senior designer position in a comparatively short time.

QUALIFICATIONS

PERSONAL: Ability to think conceptuallay. Organization and industriousness. People-orientation and tact.

PROFESSIONAL: Three-dimensional artistic ability. Color sense. A grasp of space relationships. Speaking and writing skills.

CAREER PATHS

LEVEL	JOB TITLE	EXPERIENCE NEEDED
Entry	Draftsman	College degree
2	Junior designer	1–2 years
3	Senior designer	3–5 years
4	Project manager	6–8 years
5	Partner	Additional experience and commitment

JOB RESPONSIBILITIES ♦ ENTRY LEVEL

THE BASICS: Typing and filing. Answering phones. Organizing and cataloging samples. Keeping abreast of resources and developments. Shopping sources. Learning about products and prices. Visiting showrooms. Drafting.

MORE CHALLENGING DUTIES: Developing color schemes. Sitting in on meetings with clients. Accompanying designers at installations.

Compiling presentation folders of fabrics, wallpaper, and carpet samples.

MOVING UP

Before doing original designing of interiors, you may, as a junior designer, sketch, draft, render, and possibly build small-scale models of other designers' ideas. In a store's design department you may sell and advise customers on furniture, wallpaper, and other materials.

As you improve, you'll be given projects to tackle on your own with less and less supervision. You'll have more contact with clients, discerning their needs and making recommendations. You will also oversee the work of contractors, builders, and installers to assure quality control and accuracy, and you will write your own specifications and place orders.

Demonstrated effectiveness will lead to a say in bigger, more significant decisions in space planning and layout. At this point you will outline to your client the components of the total design concept and supply price estimates for cost of labor, installations, and furnishings. You will develop an appealing and accurate presentation that will include samples, photos, models, color charts, and floor plans.

Upper-level positions will limit your time at the drawing board. You will be more involved with administration and management of others in the firm, and will meet with top-level clients. Although you will continue to develop design concepts, their execution will most likely be delegated to staff members down the line.

ADDITIONAL INFORMATION

SALARIES

Salaries, for entry-level apparel designers will be fairly low, in the $14,000 to $18,000 a year range. From that point, it's a virtual grab bag, because the size of the companies, type of product, number of designers and levels all vary greatly. A designer with a few years of experience and a successful track record for line sales can earn in excess of $45,000 a year.

In textile design, starting salaries are also in the $14,000 to $18,000 per year range. As you gain more experience and begin creating your own designs, your salary will increase. As a textile designer in an average-size firm, you can expect to earn between $25,000 to $40,000. Some free lance textile designers with a little over 2 years' experience have watched their salaries jump two or three times their starting pay.

Entry-level positions in interior design firms will pay from $17,000 to $20,000 per year. Junior designers can expect to make $18,000 to $22,000 and more a year with increasing experience. A senior designer can earn $28,000 to $40,000.

WORKING CONDITIONS

HOURS: In an industry where creativity is combined with buying and selling, standard hours are rare. Deadlines for a completion or a showing of a line, or to meet a customer's requirement or for the opening of a new office building will require design staffs to burn the midnight oil. There will be slower times as well, often after a seasonal line has been launched or a major project completed. But even then, the ambitious designer will be collecting ideas and researching trends, at work and in off hours, to prepare for the next project. For the most part, the pace is hectic, the hours are long, but the rewards are worth it!

ENVIRONMENT: In most entry-level jobs you will have your own desk, but not much other private space. Your desk or work table is likely to be in a crowded, busy design room, with phones ringing and people coming and going constantly. With promotions you will graduate to increasingly private work space.

WORKSTYLE: Most of your work will be done at your desk, but because entry-level design positions are so often supportive in nature there will be a certain amount of go-fering—shuttling back and forth between design room and showroom, shopping the stores, running errands, and visiting sites if you are working in interior design.

TRAVEL: Travel opportunities exist mostly in upper-level positions in each of the three areas of design. Once you begin dealing directly with clients and buyers, you may have to travel to many different parts of the country or even overseas to meet with them. Apparel manufacturers often contract their labor from overseas production plants, so you may make annual or frequent trips to supervise the production process and to provide concept direction. In an interior design firm your clientele may be contained in a particular city or region. Frequent contact with textile plants is a must for the textile stylist to check on color accuracy. Textile designers may also be trained for the mill supervision as well. The stylist may also travel overseas to Europe and Asia to "buy" ideas.

EXTRACURRICULAR ACTIVITIES/WORK EXPERIENCE

Creating and fitting costumes for drama and opera productions
Student membership in chapters of professional organizations
Entering design ideas in various magazine contests

INTERNSHIPS

Many production firms and design houses offer internships to students. It is beneficial to firms, enabling them to groom students for future jobs without lengthy training programs. For the student it is a valuable professional experience, an opportunity to sample a particular career and a potential job.

School placement offices in an increasing number of schools provide internship referrals to students in specific career areas. If placement services for internships are not available to you, you can do the legwork yourself. Request an appointment for an interview or write a letter to a professional in your design area, offering your services as an apprentice or intern. You may have to contact a number of people before finding someone who is willing and able to take you on, but it will be worth the effort.

RECOMMENDED READING

BOOKS
Fashion: The Inside Story, by Barbaralee Diamondstein, Rizzoli International Publications: 1985

In My Own Fashion, by Oleg Cassini, Simon and Schuster: 1987

Inside Fashion Design, Third Ed., by Sharon Tate and Mona S. Edwards, Harper & Row: 1988

PERIODICALS
Daily News Record (daily), Fairchild Publications, 7 East 12th Street, New York, NY 10003

HFD (Home Furnishings Daily) (weekly), Fairchild Publications, 7 East 12th Street, New York, NY 10003

Women's Wear Daily (daily), Fairchild Publications, 7 East 12th Street, New York, NY 10003

PROFESSIONAL ORGANIZATIONS

Amalgamated Clothing and Textile Workers Union
15 Union Square
New York, NY 10003

American Home Economics Association (AHEA)
1555 King Street
Alexandria, VA 22314

American Society of Interior Designers (ASID)

National Headquarters:
1430 Broadway, 22nd Fl.
New York, NY 10018

New York Metropolitan Chapter:
200 Lexington Avenue
New York, NY 10016

American Society of Interior Designers (ASID)

National Headquarters:
1420 Broadway
New York, NY 10018

New York Metropolitan Chapter:
950 Third Avenue, 28th Fl.
New York, NY 10022

The Fashion Group
9 Rockefeller Plaza
New York, NY 10020
(Local chapters in various cities)

International Association of Clothing Designers
240 Madison Avenue
New York, NY 10016

INTERVIEWS

SUSAN DIRIENZO
PARTNER
OFFICE PLANNING, INC.
NEW YORK, NY

I enjoy working with a firm for a long period of time. I remained for eight years at the job I had before I received my associate degree in interior design. Since school, I've been with the same interior design firm and have been promoted from junior designer to partner in two and a half years. That's unusual in this business, but I've worked very hard, put in my time, and I've grown as the company has grown.

When I began as a junior designer, I worked directly with the principal of the firm, Geraldine Vaughan. She would design a preliminary space study and I would draft it. She then would take me through the process step by step: meetings with the client; checking that specs were being met at the construction site; preparing the decorative presentation, including the selections of materials and furnishings; and working up the budget. With that concentrated experience from the beginning, I was soon ready to handle most aspects of a project on my own. Now, as partner, I manage the entire project from the first meeting with a client to the finished product. I've been learning about the business operation of the firm, in addition to developing my design experience. That's a vital aspect of my job and one I enjoy.

I have some clear-cut advice for applicants entering the field. Concentrate on and develop your drafting skills now. Drafting may seem tedious and mundane when you have a real knack for fabulous design, but do it. When you start out in a firm, a major part of your day will be spent drafting. Your accuracy and neatness, as well as your attitude, will be crucial to your future in the firm. Prepare a very professional résumé with artistic graphics and send it to the firm with a letter. When you are interviewed, your portfolio will be most significant—because you must be able to sell yourself in five minutes. Be prepared. Know how to explain your work. Keep interviewing until you find a job that suits you. Don't just accept a job because it's offered to you. Know what you want and work at finding the right position so you can use your ability.

JOANNE CIRESI
DESIGNER
OLEG CASSINI SPORTSWEAR
NEW YORK, NY

When I was in school I used to look down my nose at the volume house, mass-market apparel manufacturer, looking to begin my career with a prominent designer. Then I got my first job in one of those very volume houses through an ad in the *Daily News Record*. I started out as a design assistant in sportswear and, since the company's New York operation was small, they let me take on sales in the showroom as well. I got to meet with clients and learn what the buyers wanted. My first sportswear line was very successful because I had developed a feel for what would sell. I got to travel a lot, too—Chicago, Dallas, Seattle, Los Angeles—to meet with clients and to observe production at the company headquarters in California. The company wanted to promote me and transfer me to headquarters but I wasn't ready to leave New York. Though I could have continued upward in the New York office in a sales capacity, I realized what I really wanted was to direct my career back onto the design track.

I had to take a step down to an assistant designer position in my next job. I worked in the suit division of Bobbie Brooks, then made a lateral move within the company to designer for their Japanese licensee. Rather than design independently as in my first job, I worked with a number of other women my age who were designers for various other divisions. We were able to shop the markets, attend meetings, and provide creative feedback to one another. I really enjoyed that team camaraderie as well as the inspiration.

In the fashion business it's rare that you stay in one job for more than a few years. I don't like that aspect of the field, and sometimes wish I could stay in one company and become well established. But that's the nature of a business that continually demands new talent and creative energy.

I'm now head designer for jeans and casual sportswear at Oleg Cassini Sportswear. Since we're a separate licensee of the designer's we're a small operation, and I have many responsibilities as the only designer. Oleg Cassini comes in every few months to meet with our management, give direction and supervision to the line. I also work closely with the stylist and the merchandising staff to outline a theme or look for each season's line.

It's hectic and yet I have a lot of independence. I can work at home, shop the stores, do research at the library, and pretty much set my own hours. That gives me the freedom to put whatever I want into my job, and challenges me to do all that I can. When a line is completed, there's nothing more satisfying than seeing the fruit of my labor when the finished product comes back from production. And even better than that is learning that the line is a success in the stores!

If you're thinking of design as a career, start specializing now, whether it be in sportswear, men's wear, children's wear, tailored garments, or lingerie. Set aside your glittery visions of runway shows and couture houses, and work hard! You may think that specializing may limit your opportunities, yet specific expertise will make you much more valuable to future employers.

MIRIAM HANDELSMAN
TEXTILE DESIGNER
RITMOTEX USA
NEW YORK, NY

I got started in textile design mostly from my family because my grandfather was a textile engineer. I did a lot of weaving on my own. I went to summer school at the Rhode Island School of Design to study weaving. I also went to Italy to study weaving and it all sort of came together. When I was a studio arts major, primarily painting and drawing, at Trinity College I took a semester abroad with an international art school in Florence which I got credit for. They actually gave me college credit for weaving. I couldn't believe it.

When I came back from Italy I did a couple of internships. I did a fellowship at the Cooper-Hewitt Museum which holds the second largest collection of fabrics in the world. Although I don't think, actually, that this gave me any edge for what I'm doing now because I was working with historic fabrics, it was definitely an advantage in terms of scholarship and accomplishment. The Cooper-Hewitt does not offer fellowships anymore, but they have unpaid internships.

After college I started to work for a fabric company. I got the job through an agency that deals with textiles. Then, my grandfather of all people, who carried my résumé around with him like it was a piece of gold, gave my résumé to a friend of his who works in textiles who was willing to help me out. He hooked me up with an Italian firm, because I speak Italian, and they called me in, interviewed me, and gave me the job. It was a lot of luck and little connections.

My field is woven textiles. You have knits, you have prints, and you have wovens. I only do wovens. Since my mill is based in Italy, I am pretty much the link between the American clothing designer, because we do clothing fabrics, and the Italian mill that manufactures the fabrics. I work on the design of the fabric with the American designer so that they can have the fabric produced in Italy.

The most important thing in textile design is to meet a lot of people in the industry. With my job I have no choice but to meet people because I work with designers day-in and day-out. I have maybe five to ten appointments a day, so I am in different offices all the time—just constantly meeting people. If you can't get out to offices, you have to do the best you can to meet people. I don't think that 90% of the available jobs are advertised. It's all word of mouth, it's references from person to person. People move around in this field year to year. You've got to meet people and let them know who you are.

The skills you need depends on what area of textile design you go into, and there are a lot of different areas that demand different skills. What I do is unique since my mill is Italian. I have a lot of different responsibilities. I don't just work out designs but also have to do some selling and communicate with the technicians. I have to do all of this, mind you, in Italian. A foreign language is a real advantage because a lot of mills are not in the United States. Italian, Chinese, Japanese—actually any language you can get will give you a great advantage. This is true of the other areas in textile design because a lot of printing is done in the Orient.

You also need to be able to get along with people because you have to constantly interact with people in terms of doing your designs.

Finally, you need a really sensitive eye for color. Part of being sensitive to color is intuitive, but part of it is developed through schooling—especially the training you get in liberal arts schools, not through technical textile schools. Because you need to study painting and take color and printing classes.

The best thing to do to break into the field is to get as much textile information and knowledge as you can outside of school. If you are in a liberal arts school you will not acquire this information in your classes. If you are interested in woven fabrics, get out there and start doing research on woven fabrics. Look at how they are made. Visit mills and see how things are done. Take classes outside your college, but still go to a liberal arts college. Someone coming out of a vocational school has a narrower view of the textile industry. They have closed themselves off to other knowledge. I think they have a better base than the liberal arts graduates but they don't have the same color knowledge or knowlege of the world per se. There are excellent schools and you can avail yourself of some of their excellent classes also. If you do not have access to a fashion or design school, call a mill—get in there as much as you can.

GRAPHIC DESIGN

For people with a highly developed visual sensitivity who care not only about how something looks, but also about how appearance relates to purpose, graphic design may be an excellent career choice. The field is pivotal to the print media—books, magazines, and newspapers—which require talented designers who can give graphic expression to words and concepts, and to the advertising field, which needs artists to create the visual content of print and television advertisements. Graphic design offers a wide range of jobs—everything from laying out a tabloid newspaper, to placing the reproductions in the pages of an art book to designing a major advertising campaign.

Besides being aware of the subtly different feelings aroused by the choice of type styles and the arrangement of design elements on a page, you must have an appreciation of the content and audience of the publications or the advertisements you design. The choice of every design element—typeface, illustration, decorative features, headline placement, and even the amount of white space on a page—contributes to the ability of the publication to communicate to its readers. Each element must be carefully chosen to create an eye-catching, eye-pleasing whole.

The sharp competition among the various media is adding new challenges to the jobs of graphic artists. Newspapers are competing with television by adding special features and color graphics. Established magazines are updating their graphic images. New startups are equally aware that the look of a magazine is as important as its content. Book publishers are striving to keep up with tastes and trends in cover and interior design. As marketers have learned, buyers will judge a book (or a magazine or a newspaper) by its design. Advertisers, too, must confront an ever-changing and hard-to-please public.

The central function of the graphic designer in all publishing areas is designing the page; that is, arranging the elements of type, illustration, and so on. But important differences exist among the three industries in the pace of the work and in the materials you work with. Daily newspapers are run at breakneck speed. They're tossed away within hours of hitting the newsstands. A finely bound book of expensive art reproductions may take months to plan and design and is meant to last a lifetime or more.

In advertising, designers work on print advertisements—for magazines and newspapers, billboards, and so on—and create storyboards for television commericals. Storyboards are cartoons that show the characters, action, and camera angles of a commerical. The boards are shown to clients and, once accepted, guide those responsible for producing the commerical.

Success in this field will always depend on basic design skills and the flexibility to apply them to any new project, but the development of sophisticated microcomputer graphics is having tremendous impact on the way graphic artists do their jobs. With computer-added design, more time and effort can be spent on the creative process and much less time on developing physical models of their ideas. Page scanners, for instance, can enable designers to run an illustration through a machine that "digitizes" the image. Parts of the image can then be reshaped, moved or eliminated as the designer plays with the design. From one sketch dozens of variations can be developed. Ten or 20 approaches can be tried while working on a complicated layout and all can be stored, changed or recalled with a few keyboard strokes. This facility should allow designers to be freer and bolder in their experimentation.

JOB OUTLOOK

JOB OPENINGS WILL GROW: Faster than average

COMPETITION FOR JOBS: Keen

NEW JOB OPPORTUNITIES: Probably the fastest-growing job market for graphic designers in the 1990s will be in corporate publishing. More and more corporations are looking to bring their publishing work in-house in an effort to control costs and product quality. The development of sophisticated graphics systems is enabling companies to set up their own design studios with minimal difficulty. In these enterprises, corporations are publishing everything from sales brochures and annual reports to employee forms and internal memoranda.

GEOGRAPHIC JOB INDEX

New York, NY, Boston, MA, Chicago, IL, Washington, DC, and Los Angeles, CA, are the five cities recognized as centers of the media, but they are not the only places where graphic artists work. Newspapers are published everywhere, but job opportunties are greatest in cities large enough to support more than one daily paper and at least one Sunday/weekend paper. Any city of 100,000 people or more might be the home of substantial magazines. The greatest number of book publishing jobs are found in the five cities listed above, but publishing houses do exist in other places. New York, NY, has the highest concentration of advertising agencies, but agencies, large and small, are found in all urban areas.

WHO THE EMPLOYERS ARE

BOOK PUBLISHING jobs are most often found with the trade and paperback houses that produce a large portion of the books published in the United States. Houses that produce educational, reference, professional, and religious books may be more accessible to first-time job-hunters, though. Textbook houses are an especially good source of jobs for beginners because, unlike most publishers, they do not rely heavily on free lance designers.

MAGAZINE PUBLISHING is not limited to the mass-market consumer and news magazines that hold the central place on newsstands. Entry-level jobs are more likely found at trade magazines, which address the needs of professions (e.g., *Cable Marketing*), and at special interest magazines (e.g., *Surfing Magazine*). Don't ignore the inexpensive, picture-packed magazines of the "teen" variety, which offer some of the more challenging entry-level jobs. Corporate annual reports issued by most publicly held companies use a magazine format and are good places for beginners, as are the in-flight magazines distributed by airlines to their passengers.

NEWSPAPERS have jobs available in proportion to their circulation (the average readership). Large papers are unionized, which means they offer higher pay and more job security than nonunion papers. But small and medium-size papers, which offer more jobs to beginners, are rarely unionized. Although working conditions are not nearly as good, such papers are excellent sources of entry-level work, particularly for those graduates who need to develop basic skills.

ADVERTISING AGENCIES usually create a variety of advertising materials and are the source of the majority of job openings. Agencies come in all sizes—from one or two-person operations to large companies employing 1000 or more people. In-house advertising departments are another source of employment. Rather than pay an independent agency to handle all their advertising needs, many major corporations handle some of their advertising work in-house.

MAJOR EMPLOYERS

TRADE BOOK PUBLISHERS
Doubleday & Company, New York, NY
Little, Brown & Company, Boston, MA

Macmillian Publishing Company, New York, NY
Random House, New York, NY
Simon and Schuster, New York, NY

PAPERBACK PUBLISHERS
Ballantine Books, New York, NY
Bantam Books, New York, NY
Dell Books, New York, NY
Penguin Books, New York, NY
Warner Books, New York, NY

TEXTBOOK AND PROFESSIONAL BOOK PUBLISHERS
Houghton Mifflin Company, Boston, MA
McGraw-Hill, Inc., New York, NY
Prentice-Hall, Englewood Cliffs, NJ
Scott, Foresman, Glenview, IL
John Wiley and Sons, New York, NY

RELIGIOUS BOOK PUBLISHERS
Abington Press, Nashville, TN
Baker Bookhouse, Grand Rapids, MI
Paulist Press, Mahwah, NJ
The Westminster Press, Philadelphia, PA
Zondervan, Grand Rapids, MI

CONSUMER MAGAZINE PUBLISHERS
Condé Nast Magazines, New York, NY
Hearst Publications, New York, NY
Meredith Corp., Des Moines, IA
News America Publishing, New York, NY
Ziff-Davis Publishing Co., New York, NY

TRADE MAGAZINE PUBLISHERS
Chilton Co., Radnor, PA
Fairchild Publications, New York, NY

CMP Publications, Manhasset, NY
Harcourt Brace Jovanovich, New York, NY
Penton Publications Inc., Cleveland, OH

LARGE CIRCULATION NEWSPAPERS
The Chicago Tribune, Chicago, Il
The Detroit News, Detroit, MI
The Los Angeles Times, Los Angeles, CA
The New York Daily News, New York, NY
The New York Post, New York, NY
The New York Times, New York, NY
The Philadelphia Inquirer, Philadelphia, PA
USA Today, Washington, DC
The Wall Street Journal, New York, NY
The Washington Post, Washington, DC

MAJOR ADVERTISING AGENCIES
Backer Spielvogel Bates Worldwide Inc., New York, NY
BBDO Worldwide Inc., New York, NY
D'Arcy Masius Benton & Bowles Inc., New York, NY
Doyle Dane Bernbach International Inc., New York, NY
Foote, Cone & Belding, Chicago, IL
J. Walter Thompson Company, New York, NY
Leo Burnett Company Inc., Chicago, IL
Lintas Worldwide, New York, NY
McCann-Erickson Worldwide, New York, NY
Ogilvy & Mather Worldwide Inc., New York, NY
Saatchi & Saatchi Worldwide Inc., New York, NY
Young & Rubicam Inc., New York, NY

HOW TO BREAK INTO THE FIELD

It is often difficult for recent grads to land a starting position. To get
your first break, take any summer, part-time, or internship jobs you
can find. At the entry level, the most important skills are technical,

not creative. In other words, you execute a layout, but you may not design it. With luck you may find a first job that allows you the opportunity to build a professional design portfolio, more realistically, you'll get some exposure to art department functions and demonstrate that you can make neat mechanicals.

To arrange an interview, send a letter and résumé to the head of the art department, and follow up with a phone call. You might be invited to interview if your qualifications are appropriate. You will be expected to show your portfolio at the interview. Make it the best possible introduction to your talents.

Your portfolio should feature your own design strengths and interests; it should also include any mechanicals you have done and should stress any special skills you have—in typography, for example. Besides showing what you can do now, the portfolio should show that you are creative and intelligent and that you will be able to learn and grow to meet the design challenges that eventually will come your way.

At the interview, your prospective employer will want to see that you have thought about your interest and abilities and about your long-term goals. Do you think your strengths lie in typography or illustration? Are you more interested in print advertising or television storyboards? The more self-assessment you have done, the better impression you will make. You should also demonstrate that you are willing and able to perform basic skills and are eager to learn. Whatever job you apply for—whether in the print media or in advertising—make sure you learn something about the operations and objectives of the industry before the interview.

INTERNATIONAL JOB OPPORTUNITIES

Design may be an international language, but aspiring graphic artists will have difficulty finding jobs with foreign publications. Highly qualified professionals may be able to work abroad, and graphic artists have successfully free lanced in other countries, but the opportunities for overseas work are few and far between.

GRAPHIC DESIGN ENTREPRENEURIAL

For many who enter the graphic design field, the career path they choose turns out to be a road to independence. In many ways, free lancing is a perfect fit for the graphics design profession. For graphic designers, a free lance career affords the opportunity to explore a virtually limitless variety of creative venues—designing an advertising brochure one day, creating a design for a book cover the next day, building an illustration for a magazine piece the following day, and so on. For companies that need the services of graphic designers, having a pool of free lancers to choose from means a steady stream of new and creative solutions to design questions.

The portfolio is the graphic designer's most important tool when it comes to finding and securing new work. Portfolios must be built carefully, being constantly updated and changed as the designer's range of experience and skill grows. In time, a portfolio will grow from an all-inclusive collection of works to a "best of" representation that shows an experienced designer's most impressive work.

For graphic designers, striking out on a free lance career doesn't require a great deal of financial investment. You need your tools of the trade, of course. Increasingly, that also means buying a graphics-oriented microcomputer, but you can set up shop in your home. One quality that's essential is patience. New businesses are always a risky venture, and usually it takes a couple of years to build a solid base of clients that provide steady work. If you can endure a few years of financial sacrifice—and if you're good enough—you could very well establish an independent business that thrives for years.

THE WORK

In any publishing establishment, the design or art department does not stand alone but constantly interacts with other departments. In book publishing, designers receive direction from the editorial department, which works with authors to ready manuscripts for publication, and from the sales and marketing departments, which sell the finished product. These divisions of the publishing house have as direct an interest in the appearance of a finished book as the graphic designers.

Interior and jacket design are usually two distinct functions. For the jacket or cover of trade and paperback books the designer must create a visual concept that attracts the buyer and gives a feeling of the contents of the book. The interior designer selects the type (and there are hundreds of distinctive styles), its size, and the placement of the copy on the page, and designs chapter headings, the title page, and other internal visual elements. Special challenges arise in art or children's books, where the design has greater weight than in a novel, for example. In larger houses, such books may be handled by special design staffs.

At magazines, art departments, organization, and individual job duties vary, depending on the needs of the particular publication. A magazine with few illustrations or a relatively simple design presents a far different challenge from a heavily illustrated publication or one that strives for a highly "graphic" look. The artist designs the features, making all decisions conform to the magazine's format, which is set by the art director. The designer coordinates the arrangement of photos, illustrations, and copy, and designs heading and other decorative features. In consultation with the editorial, advertising, and production departments, the design department puts together the "book" of the magazine by arranging the features and advertisements. Because the cover is often the most important selling feature of a magazine, the design department may not have complete control over its selection. Rather, the cover illustration or photo may be chosen by the publisher or the managing editor, often in consultation with marketing personnel.

Newspaper designers operate in a strict format and take their direction in the placement of news stories from the managing editor. The designer does not decide which stories belong on page one or in section B, but he or she does arrange them. Photos must also be chosen and placed on the page, and charts, graphs, and maps are created as needed. The design staff may also design advertisements for local advertisers, a service much appreciated by smaller businesses. Special weekly and Sunday features give scope for design that approaches a magazine's style. Some staffers may work full time on such features at large circulation papers.

In advertising agencies, artists work in the creative department, which also includes copywriters. The creative department looks to the account services personnel, who work directly with the clients, for information about products and guidance in planning a campaign. Being a competent artist (or even an exceptional one) is not enough; you must always please the client. The advertising industry offers less security than most other media. When an agency loses a major client, those who worked on that account are often let go. The pressure to meet a client's needs—even if it means late hours and strict deadlines—is constant.

The course of an individual career is hard to predict. Many experienced graphic designers free lance. Even artists with full-time jobs will broaden their professional experience (and supplement their incomes) by doing extra work on the side. Some professionals move between these industries, particularly at the early stages of their careers.

QUALIFICATIONS

PERSONAL: Attention to detail. Ability to meet deadlines. Ability to work in a group. Ability to communicate your ideas and impressions in words and images. Sensitivity to and keen interest in current trends and tastes.

PROFESSIONAL: An appreciation of writing, whether it is fiction, nonfiction, or journalism. The ability to read carefully and to translate your responses into visual terms. Some familiarity with the operations of a publishing establishment. Knowledge of typography and production processes.

CAREER PATHS

LEVEL	JOB TITLE	EXPERIENCE NEEDED
Entry	Apprentice, design assistant	College degree. Portfolio. Layout/design experience preferred
2	Junior or assistant designer	6 months to 1 year or longer, depending on experience and background
3	Staff artist, associate art director, senior designer, section designer (newspaper)	5–8 years
4	Art director, managing art director	10 + years

JOB RESPONSIBILITIES ♦ ENTRY LEVEL

THE BASICS: Making paste-ups and mechanicals to a designer's specifications. Keeping track of projects assigned to free lancers. Developing skills in photo retouching and chart making, especially at newspapers. Ordering supplies.

MORE CHALLENGING DUTIES: Minor design projects. Meeting with writers, artists, and editors. Putting finishing touches on free lance work. The smaller the organization, the sooner you may be given more challenging work; opportunities to try your hand at design will open during rush periods or when you fill in for absent staffers.

MOVING UP

Once you have mastered basic skills, you can begin to do actual design. At first you will be given limited projects, and your work will be closely supervised, but as you prove your abilities, you will be given more independence. In book publishing, you will deal with editors and marketing staff to assess their expectations and sell your own ideas. In magazines and with special newspaper features, you will design sections of the publication. You will be required to follow the publisher's basic format, but this format should provide room to express your own ideas. When you work with basic newspaper copy, you will be expected to design quickly and conform to basic guidelines. A sense of teamwork, which is part of any staff position, is particularly important in advertising. You must constantly contribute your skills and ideas to any campaign on which you work.

With considerable design achievement and a demonstration of managerial skills, you may move into the position of assistant art director and, later, art director. Art directors are less involved in actual design. They are responsible for monitoring their staffs and ensuring that a consistent standard of quality is maintained. They review all design work, suggesting changes or rejecting graphics that they find unacceptable, and they hire free lancers, photographers, and illustrators. The director acts as the liaison between the art department and other departments, such as the editorial staff in a publishing house, or the account executives in an ad agency, and deals with suppliers and printers.

Whatever your job—whether it is directing the designers, doing the design yourself, or simply pasting up someone else's design— one of the joys of graphic design is that the fruits of your labor are soon seen on the newsstands or in the bookstores.

ADDITIONAL INFORMATION

SALARIES

Salaries for graphic artists in all four of these industries are roughly equal. An entry-level artist can expect to earn between $15,000 and $18,000 a year. With five years' experience compensation can rise to between $23,000 and $35,000; with ten years' experience to an excess of $40,000.

WORKING CONDITIONS

HOURS: At many magazines, book publishers, and advertising agencies, ten to six are normal hours, although the time you work varies with deadline pressures. At major newspapers, designers work an early shift, mechanicals people work later shifts. Saturday and Sunday work is possible. Weekly papers have one traditionally late night—usually Thursday—the day before the paper comes out. At any employer, the smaller the department, the less specialized the work becomes, and the more you can expect to work overtime.

ENVIRONMENT: At books and magazines, shared offices and bullpen arrangements are common. The most luxurious quarters are normally found at picture magazines, where the value of the graphics takes precedence over most other elements. Newspaper design departments are open and noisy. The comfort of advertising offices depends on the size of the agency or department.

WORKSTYLE: The day is spent at the drawing board. Inter-office meetings offer an occasional change of pace. Entry-level people may be required to do basic clerical duties, but these are not a part of every beginning job.

TRAVEL: The artist's job does not include travel, except perhaps for department heads, who may attend conferences or sales meetings.

EXTRACURRICULAR ACTIVITIES/WORK EXPERIENCE

Campus publications: design and layout
Summer or part-time experience at a book, magazine or newspaper publisher (even a job that does not involve design or layout will give you an idea of how these businesses operate)

INTERNSHIPS

Because of the cost of equipment and the space required to set up a drawing table, internships are less common in the art department than in other areas of publishing. They are quite rare in book publishing. Those internships that are available are found primarily at larger magazines and newspapers. Nevertheless, try to talk your way into an internship. If you have some experience, perhaps from layout work on a campus publication, you may have a chance. Write directly to the art directors of publications that interest you, carefully explaining your qualifications. Another source of experience is the throwaway newspapers that cover news and events in small towns or city neighborhoods. They are free and are financed by advertising revenues. These papers will not be able to pay you, but they may be more willing to train you in the basics than other publications. If you are interested in advertising, offer your services to small, local agencies.

RECOMMENDED READING

BOOKS
Design career, by Steven Heller and Seymour Chwast, Van Nostrand Reinhold: 1987

Design Career: Practical Knowledge for Beginning Illustrators and Graphic Designers, Push Pin Editions: 1987

Graphic Design Career Guide, by Steven Heller, Watson-Guptill: 1983

Literary Marketplace, R.R. Bowker Co.: revised annually

Magazine Marketplace, R.R. Bowker Co.: revised annually

Opportunities in Commercial Art and Graphic Design, by Barbara Gordon, National Textbook Co.: 1987

Standard Directory of Advertising Agencies, National Register Publishing Co.: revised three times each year

PERIODICALS

Adweek (weekly), Adweek Publications, 49 East 21st Street, New York, NY 10010 (regional editions for south-east, west, south-west and mid-west)

Editor and Publisher: The Fourth Estate (weekly), 11 West 19th Street, New York, NY 10011

Folio: The Magazine for Magazine Management, 6 River Bend, P.O. Box 4949, Stamford, CT 06907

Print (bimonthly), 104 5th Avenue, New York, NY 10011

Publishers Weekly (weekly), Cahrer's Publishing (division of Reed Publishing), 245 West 17th Street, New York, NY 10011

PROFESSIONAL ASSOCIATIONS

American Association of Advertising Agencies
666 Third Avenue
New York, NY 10017

The Graphic Artists Guild
11 West 20th Street, 8th Fl.
New York, NY 10011

Society of Publication Designers
60 East 42nd Street, Ste. 1416
New York, NY 10165

INTERVIEWS

KARI HAYDEN
DESIGNER
COMMUNICATIONS DEPARTMENT
NEW ENGLAND MUTUAL LIFE INSURANCE
BOSTON, MA

I first got a B.F.A. After I graduated I interviewed for several jobs. The way I found this job was through a friend who had worked at the company I had previously worked for. She was director of the design department here and she hired me.

Basically, I do a lot of desk-top publishing. With that system I design brochures, newsletters, invitations, posters, advertisements, and a whole array of other things. There really are no boundaries. But in general I help design anything that is printed.

The best way to move up in this field is to have a lot of design talent. It also depends on what kind of education you've had. You should also continue to educate yourself—go to conferences, learn what is being done in the field, find out about the new and different systems and software in desk-top publishing. You have to have a really good understanding of design. You also need good communication skills, because you need to present your ideas to upper management. At the same time, you must be able to manage people and work with them as a team.

What is really strange in design is that almost every job requires a BFA, but an MFA doesn't really help at all. In fact it is the equivalent of a BFA. I find that very surprising. Unless, of course, you've gone to Yale or the Basil School of Design. I know several people who have MFAs and it really doesn't matter. Employers pay more attention to your portfolio, what type of person you are, and how you communicate. They care if you have a good understanding of visual communication and if you will be able to determine the client's needs. You also need artistic talent, like a sense of color. I found that education helped me to develop my artistic talents even more—my sense of typography and how to make things more legible. I think that it is also important to both pay attention to details and also look at the big picture.

I would advise someone trying to break into the field to go to a good school that has a good reputation in design or fine arts. Very few people come into the business without this background. If a person doesn't have this educational background it's a lot harder. I do know somebody who has a degree in sociology, but she's very rare. I saw her portfolio after she took a few classes and I wouldn't even know where to direct her as far as a job. I wouldn't feel comfortable about referring her to any of my contacts and felt bad about that, but the field is specialized in that respect. You just need the background to develop the skills you need as a designer. I would take some classes in design and see if you have the ability and if you like it. Basically, the way you get your first design job is through your portfolio. Your portfolio represents who you are and the way you think and it shows your skills. This is what you need to get a full-time or a free lance job. Essentially, you need to build up a portfolio.

MICHAEL CHESWORTH
ART DIRECTOR
WALKER & COMPANY
NEW YORK, NY

I started drawing cartoons when I was in high school and selling them to local university publications. Then I went to engineering school for two years at Penn State and dropped out. I went out west and got a job as a medical illustrator in a hospital. I decided from there to go to art school and be an artist. I came to New York to, I hoped, get the best education I could get in art. I went to Parsons School of Design and decided I wanted to work in books. So I got a job with a big publisher in New York even before I graduated from Parsons. I was a full-time free lance artist which means I just went in and they paid me, but I didn't have any benefits. I could sort of control my own schedule. After a year and half of that they promoted me to assistant art director, which was a regular full-time staff job. From there I saw an advertisement in the paper for a job at Walker Publishing and I applied. They looked at my portfolio and I got the job.

We basically come up with ideas for the book jackets. We talk with the editors and ask them what the book's about. Theoretically, we also talk to the sales people and find out what a good way would be to sell the book. The jacket design has a decent amount to do with sales. In fact, that's really the only reason to have it on there. Then we try to put a jacket on the book that's nice looking, interesting, and represents the book as best as possible. Inside all of that we throw in some art, some design, and try to do something that's really snappy. From there we do a rough sketch that is more or less just for my team, which is myself and my two assistants. From the rough sketch we go to something we call a comp, or comprehensive sketch, which is a very tight sketch, usually in color. We show this to the editor, the managing editor who is in charge, and we show it to the sales people. Everybody gets to look at it and they put their comments on it. If we get this approved we go on to do a mechanical, which is what the printer uses to make the jacket. This also has to be approved, so there's a lot of back and forth between us and the other people here. It's a group effort but we're the ones who physically do the artwork.

Also, we do the interiors of the books. There is not much room here for doing anything crazy. The emphasis is on clarity, but it can be interesting. For each book we also do a design on the inside—the kind of type, the size of the type, how much type is on a page.

In a certain sense you don't really need to go to school to become a graphic designer, as you would if you wanted to be a lawyer, because no one ever asks to see your diploma once you graduate from art school. They really just want to see your portfolio, which is your best work in a folder. You show that to someone and you say this is what I've done. If they like it, they hire you. The best way to get started, as far as I'm concerned, is to get a staff job—a job where you are working for a specific company, because if you do not have a lot of commercial background you are not going to be as desirable in a free lance situation. A lot of graphic designers who have acquired the necessary skills and compiled a decent portfolio work as free lancers. As a free lancer you usually do a specific job and get paid a specific amount of money. For instance, a lot of people in New York do book jackets free lance—they just do one book jacket at a time. They work at home and rather than being on salary they have job after job after job after job throughout the year. They run around with their portfolios, meet different people and try to get work. They are half salesmen and half craftsmen. Anybody can do this—you don't need a degree, but you do learn a lot in school.

In New York people tend to change companies in order to move up. You can get promoted within a large company. Often, when you get a job in a small company you can't go anywhere. At my present job there's nowhere to move up, but this is a good position for me as art director. If I wanted to enhance my career somehow, I would either move to a larger company, more prestigious company, or I would free lance and just do the work I specifically want to do and sell that. However, that is a lot of work and you have to hustle around a lot.

If you want to move up you have to have a really good portfolio. Your résumé is also really important if you want to get into management. It would be important for me to be able to show my progression from being a free lance designer, to being an assistant art director, to being an art director. If you want to change jobs there are a couple of things you can do. You can go to a headhunter. When you get to a certain level in your career this is useful. If you're young and inexperienced this is a waste of time because the head-hunter makes money off the salary you get. When you're young you're not going to make any kind of salary that's going to do anything for a headhunter. I've had some bad experiences with headhunters but then again that's probably because I was not very experienced.

You can look at the paper and also word of mouth helps. There are also publications, like *Publishers Weekly*, for our profession that have classifieds. I know in Boston, *Ad Week* carries art positions, and *The New York Times* always has a slew of art jobs. If you want to get free lance work you should look at the book *The Artist's Market* which businesses list in, describe what they want, and what they pay.

If you are interested in design you should have an interest in art per se. The really good designers and the really good illustrators all have a real interest in art, fine art. It's not a high paying field like going into banking or becoming a lawyer. If you are interested in money—don't go into this field. You really have to love art. You have to be willing to compromise which is not easy because most artists tend to work on their own. No one ever tells them what color to put down. But you have to do that in commercial art—you have to be able to work with other people.

I would tell an aspiring commercial artist to draw a lot. Draw anything—that's the best way to learn. Pay attention to what's going on in the graphic arts world—look at magazines, look at books, look at everything. Also, look at art history to get a feel for the whole flow of art through the ages up to now. Don't be afraid to talk to professionals. If you're interested, you can always write a letter to a graphic artist and ask if you can come and talk about the field. I've found that people are very helpful. People you would think are too busy to talk are usually interested in helping young people.

MAGAZINE PUBLISHING

The magazine industry may well be the best-kept secret in publishing. You may think this statement is stretching a point more than a little; after all, most people are well aware of glossy, high-profile publications like *Time*, *Newsweek*, *Cosmopolitan*, *People*, and *Sports Illustrated*. The fact is, however, that the magazines you see at a typical newsstand represent only a small fraction of the magazines published in the U.S. For every "glamour" publication like *Vogue* and *Esquire*, there are a large handful of magazines with names like *Modern Grocer* and *Microwaves & Radio Frequency*.

Magazines generally fall into two categories: consumer publications and trade publications. Consumer magazines are those that you'd find on sale at a newsstand. They include general-interest titles like *Time* and special-interest titles like *Byte*, a magazine for computer users, and *Gourmet*, a magazine for food enthusiasts. Trade publications cater to much more specific audiences—typically, they focus on a specific business or profession.

The magazine business is indeed mercurial, a fact that holds both good and bad news for job seekers. A hot new trend can spawn dozens of new magazines and a wealth of job opportunities. Once that trend cools, those jobs can disappear quickly. The home-computer boom of the early 1980s led to the creation of more than a score of magazines for computer buyers and users. Within five years, most of those magazines folded.

Despite the apparent risks involved in the business, however, the number of magazines being published continues to grow. That's because the financial rewards for success are great. In trade-magazine publishing, for example, net profit margins of 20 percent or greater are not uncommon. For every magazine that fails, it seems, another two are started to take its place.

The potential for big profits and losses has fostered another trend in publishing: changes in ownership. Mergers, acquisitions, and buyouts are a fact of life in magazine publishing, as they are in book publishing. Magazine publishing empires can be created or dismantled seemingly overnight. Less than a decade ago, McGraw-Hill, Inc., boasted a massive magazine-publishing operation that included some 70 trade and consumer titles. The company has since sold off most of those titles and now publishes fewer than 10. Rupert Murdoch, the Australian publishing magnate, spent the better part of the 1970s and early 1980s building a magazine-publishing empire in the U.S.—and then set out to reshape that empire, selling off major publications like *New York* for even bigger properties, like *TV Guide*.

Although the job market in magazine publishing is highly competitive, many opportunities exist, even at the entry level. The greater number of magazines being published, combined with a leveling off or decrease in the number of college graduates looking to start a career in publishing, has led to an opening up of the market. Entry-level positions in editorial, production, and sales are available. The best bet for new job seekers is to focus their searches in the New York and Boston areas. However, magazine publishers have offices in many other areas nationwide.

JOB OUTLOOK

JOB OPENINGS WILL GROW: As fast as average

COMPETITION FOR JOBS: Keen

Expect the most competition for jobs in editorial departments; production and circulation departments are more accessible. If you're considering sales, you stand a much better chance of finding a sales trainee position at a lesser-known magazine.

NEW JOB OPPORTUNITIES

Special-interest magazines are the backbone of the industry; the reading public has resoundingly demonstrated its acceptance of the better narrow-subject magazines that have appeared in ever increasing numbers in recent years. If you have the vision to pick the genre of magazine that will be the next hot trend and find a place in the startup of one of these publications, you can get your career off to a fast start. A knowledge of computerized typesetting gained through a summer job or internship can be a great help in landing a good position in the production department.

GEOGRAPHIC JOB INDEX

Editorial offices are located in and around five major metropolitan areas, which are, in order of size, New York, NY, Washington, DC, Chicago, IL, Los Angeles, CA, and Boston, MA. Sales representatives occasionally work out of their homes or in small satellite offices across the country.

WHO THE EMPLOYERS ARE

The most coveted positions are with well-known news and mass-market consumer magazines, such as *Time* and *Glamour*. You'll find it easier to get your foot in the door with special-interest magazines such as *Personal Computing*, or trade publications, such as *Plastics Technology*. Association and organization magazines and Sunday newspaper supplements are other possibilities.

MAJOR EMPLOYERS

MAJOR PUBLISHERS OF CONSUMER MAGAZINES
Condé Nast, New York, NY
Diamandis Communications, New York, NY

Hearst Magazines, New York, NY
Meredith Corporation, Des Moines, IA
News America Publishing Inc., New York, NY
Readers Digest Association, Pleasantville, NY
Time, Inc., New York, NY
Times Mirror Magazines, Inc., New York, NY
Ziff-Davis, New York, NY

MAJOR PUBLISHERS OF TRADE MAGAZINES
Chilton Company, Radnor, PA
Fairchild Publications, New York, NY
McGraw-Hill, Inc., New York, NY
Petersen Publishing Company, Los Angeles, CA

HOW TO BREAK INTO THE FIELD

If you're resourceful enough to land an internship or summer
position at a magazine, you'll have an edge over other job candidates
when you graduate, because you've already been able to show the
people above you what you can do. Barring that, try for personal
contact with someone who can hire you or recommend you for
hiring. Attending one of the three best-known summer publishing
institutes provides opportunities to meet such people.

For more information, write to the directors.

New York University's
Summer Publishing Institute
Center for Publishing
48 Cooper Square
New York NY 10003

Radcliffe College/Harvard Univ.
Radcliffe Publishing Course
6 Ash Street
Cambridge, MA 02138

An additional suggestion for getting into magazine publishing is to send a well-thought-out and carefully written letter to the editor-in-chief or head of the department of the magazine for which you want to work. Remember, unless your letter and résumé are outstanding, they will simply be funneled to the personnel department. Employment agencies specializing in publishing placement are worth a try, as are help-wanted ads in newspapers and trade magazines, although with the latter you'll encounter the most competition.

ENTREPRENEURIAL

As with book publishing, the coming of the computer age has opened the door for would-be publishers to start their own magazines. As with books, these entrepreneurs usually don't have the financial resources to take on the industry's heavyweights. But a number of success stories have been penned by individuals who have parlayed some publishing experience, the knowledge of a specific business or subject, and a properly equipped electronic publishing system to produce worthwhile, albeit small-scale, publications. One magazine, called *Personal Publishing*, is produced by an entrepreneurial publisher for other budding publishers. Bill James, a writer of a series of best-sellers about baseball, started his publishing career by putting together his own newsletter.

A less risky but potentially rewarding entrepreneurial path involves free lance services. As in other businesses, magazine publishers, particularly small publishers of which there are many, try to operate with minimal staffing levels. To compensate, they use outside help to get their magazines out. Experienced free lance writers are in high demand, and should continue to be in the near future. High-prestige magazines like *Vanity Fair* now pay as much as $10,000 or more for stories from top writers. Of course, the vast majority of free lancers make far less than that, but fees are generally increasing. Demand for free lance copyediting, proofreading, and production services is also growing.

EDITORIAL

The editorial effort of developing an article, column, or feature from an idea to finished copy is an involved one. It begins with the discussion of an idea for a new project or story at a regular meeting of the editorial staff. The idea may originate with in-house editors or outside free lancers. Once an idea is approved, editors and their assistants work with a writer to refine and focus it for their readership and to review the finished manuscript for content and style. Editors often cultivate an area of expertise, such as food, travel, fashion, or electronics, and may produce monthly sections or columns on that topic. An editorial job often also requires working with designers, illustrators, or photographers to develop the visual side of an article.

QUALIFICATIONS

PERSONAL: Good command of English. Ability to write well and recognize good writing. A creative spirit. Ability to spot new trends and ideas.

PROFESSIONAL: Typing (40 words per minute or better). Proofreading skills. Familiarity with word processing helpful but not essential. Good phone manner. Some knowledge of printing and production a plus.

CAREER PATHS

LEVEL	JOB TITLE	EXPERIENCE NEEDED
Entry	Editorial assistant, Researcher	College degree
2	Assistant editor, Staff writer	1–4 years
3	Associate editor, Department editor	5–7 years
4	Senior editor	7–10 years
5	Executive editor, Managing editor, Editor-in-chief	10+ years

JOB RESPONSIBILITIES ♦ ENTRY LEVEL

THE BASICS: Answering phones. Typing manuscripts and correspondence. Making copies. Filing. Sending contracts to writers.

MORE CHALLENGING DUTIES: Attending press conferences. Doing basic research. Writing short articles. Reviewing unsolicited manuscripts. Developing new article ideas.

MOVING UP

While you master the routine work of being an assistant, be prepared for any opportunity to let your talents shine. At a formal meeting or in casual conversations, don't miss a chance to make your contribution. As you progress, you may find yourself more involved with writing or editing, depending on your skills and preferences. Increasingly, your ability to produce consistently good copy on demand will be a prerequisite to upward mobility. Once you are more established, you'll have the luxury of being able to write in your areas of interest or expertise.

There is more status and power involved in being an editor, but few editors spend much time writing articles. They're more apt to be discussing ideas with writers, polishing copy, writing blurbs and headlines for the pieces they've directed, and working with the art department on story layout. Senior editors will devote their efforts to editing and supervising major stories or whole sections of the publication.

ADVERTISING SALES/MARKETING

Pick up any popular magazine and you can't help noticing the ads. Ads take up as much as half the page space for a very simple reason—ad income provides at least half of the revenue of most magazines.

The job of a magazine sales staff is to sell ad space. Magazine sales people spend much of their time talking to account executives and media planners at ad agencies and at companies whose business they want to cultivate. As a salesperson, you have to convince a potential client that the demographics of your readership match the desired audience. You'll use readership studies and surveys prepared by your magazine and by the industry to prove your point. You'll also have to research the client's needs by pulling relevant statistics and information from research done about the particular product or service your potential client wants to promote.

The marketing, or sales promotion department, works with sales to develop strategies and provide information that will help the sales staff increase business. The career description below is geared more toward sales because the majority of jobs are there, rather than in marketing or promotion.

The most successful magazines seldom take on beginners in their sales departments. You must first develop a track record at less well-established publications.

QUALIFICATIONS

PERSONAL: Outgoing personality. Good conversationalist. Ability to influence others. Follow through and persistence. Disposition to cope with rejection and not take the word *no* personally.

PROFESSIONAL: Ability to work comfortably with numbers. Understanding of basic business and management concepts. Sales experience preferred for sales jobs.

CAREER PATHS

LEVEL	JOB TITLE	EXPERIENCE NEEDED
Entry	Sales assistant, sales trainee, or secretary	College degree. Sales experience useful

2	Sales representative	1–3 years
3	District or group sales manager	3–7 years
4	Advertising manager	7–10 years
5	Publisher	10–15+ years

JOB RESPONSIBILITIES ♦ ENTRY LEVEL

THE BASICS: Answering telephones. Typing letters. Filing contracts. Sending information to potential clients.

MORE CHALLENGING DUTIES: Writing letters to potential clients. Learning to put together and give presentations. Accompanying more senior people on sales calls. Researching information about prospective clients and their products.

MOVING UP

You must demonstrate the subtle combination of assertiveness and tact that wins advertising dollars. A solid record of successful sales leads to your being assigned larger and tougher accounts. Most of your dealings will be with advertising agencies, which represent individual clients, rather than with the advertisers themselves.

Managers of sales and marketing departments are more concerned with the overall patterns of advertising income and ensuring that the right page space is available for each client. A creative advertising director, who knows the strengths of the publication and can cultivate lasting relationships with dependable advertisers, can make or break a magazine.

CIRCULATION

Without the circulation department, which gets the product to the consumer, the efforts of every other staffer on the magazine would be pointless. This department oversees subscription and newsstand sales. Because advertising rates are based on the average number of copies sold and read, the size of the circulation determines how much money the publication takes in. The key to success is subscriber renewal—dependable readers who will keep buying for years. The high expense of attracting new subscribers can be justified only if circulation has researched and carefully targeted its potential market. Circulation is also responsible for overseeing subscription fulfillment and for collecting overdue bills and canceling unpaid subscriptions.

If you work in circulation, you must understand the publication's readership and devise ways of reaching more people with similar interests and tastes. However, the circulation department does not influence editorial decisions—you must work with the product as it is, however tempting it might be to suggest ways of increasing its popularity.

Career opportunities in circulation vary, depending on the size and setup of the publishing house. The majority of magazine circulation jobs are in subscription, which always is based in-house. Because so few recent graduates consider going into circulation, you stand a good chance of finding a position in this department if you demonstrate a genuine interest in it.

QUALIFICATIONS

PERSONAL: Well organized. Detail-oriented. Able to work well independently.

PROFESSIONAL: Awareness of magazine market trends and readership. Computer skills helpful.

CAREER PATHS

LEVEL	JOB TITLE	EXPERIENCE NEEDED
Entry	Circulation assistant	College degree
2	Manager of collections, renewal, or fulfillment	3–5 years
3	Assistant director of circulation	5–7 years
4	Circulation director	7–10 years

JOB RESPONSIBILITIES ♦ ENTRY LEVEL

THE BASICS: Clerical duties, filing, and typing. Updating customer files. Handling subscriber complaints.

MORE CHALLENGING DUTIES: Assisting senior staffers. Handling long lists and many facts and figures.

MOVING UP

As much as any salesperson, you must believe in the value of your product. As you move up you might specialize in an area, such as fulfillment, or become involved in the promotional end of circulation, such as direct mail campaigns. The circulation director oversees both subscription and newsstand sales, the latter through either an outside distribution firm or in-house staff.

PRODUCTION

Although magazines are sometimes typeset and always printed outside the company, an in-house staff directs and oversees production work. Besides choosing materials, suppliers, printers, and binders, the production department establishes and enforces schedules for the editorial department. Missed deadlines can increase costs. Production oversees each issue from printer to binder to distributor and subscriber. To complicate this task, magazines are printed in sections, often at printing plants far removed from one another and the magazine's office.

Although you won't have a hand in the writing and illustration, production work does involve talent of a different kind. You must see that the efforts of the editorial and art departments are combined into an attractive, organized whole that communicates the editorial stance of the magazine. You also need a good head for figures and finances, a knowledge of printing materials, and the processes of graphic reproduction. Personality and temperament count for a great deal, because you must be able to handle emergencies and resolve last-minute crises before deadline.

QUALIFICATIONS

PERSONAL: Ability to handle pressure and deadlines. Creative sensibility. Commitment to quality. Diplomacy in dealing with others.

PROFESSIONAL: An eye for detail. Proofreading and organizational skills. Meticulous record-keeping. An understanding of graphic reproduction and printing techniques.

CAREER PATHS

LEVEL	JOB TITLE	EXPERIENCE NEEDED
Entry	Production or traffic assistant	College degree
2	Layout coordinator	2 years
3	Production manager	12 years
4	Production director	15 + years

JOB RESPONSIBILITIES ♦ ENTRY LEVEL

THE BASICS: Typing, filing, keeping a dummy book. Traffic assistants have some clerical duties unique to this area: handling the flow of layouts, proofs, and other documents necessary to production.

MORE CHALLENGING DUTIES: Some responsibilities for planning production work and handling customer service (e.g. an angry advertiser who didn't like the way an ad looked in print). The opportunity to observe all facets of the production process and become knowledgeable about the different suppliers and manufacturers and the quality of their work.

MOVING UP

More senior people are responsible for arranging contracts, setting budgets and schedules, and keeping the entire operation running. The production director has the ultimate responsibility for the quality of the published product and for seeing that it comes out on time. This individual also must approve and implement any new technological processes.

ADDITIONAL INFORMATION

SALARIES

Salaries in all positions vary widely depending on the size and type of publication and an individual's experience. The following ranges are typical of the latest magazine salaries:

EDITORIAL

Editorial assistant	$16,800 to $18,000
Assistant editor	$22,000 to $24,000
Department editor	$34,200 to $38,400
Senior editor	$40,000 to $60,000
Executive editor	$50,000 to $75,000

ADVERTISING SALES/MARKETING

Sales representative (beginning)	$25,000 to $35,000
Advertising manager	$46,000 to $72,000
Advertising director	$52,000 to $80,000

CIRCULATION

Circulation assistant	$18,000 to $21,000
Assistant director	$25,000 to $29,000
Circulation director	$40,000 and up

PRODUCTION

Production assistant	$16,000 to $19,000
Layout coordinator	$25,000 to $30,000
Production manager	$29,000 to $45,000
Production director	$35,000 and up

WORKING CONDITIONS

HOURS: In editorial and production, expect to put in overtime as deadlines approach. In sales, visits and calls to clients are made between nine and five, although there are often after-work functions to attend. In all areas, expect to work more than a 40-hour week and to bring work home if you plan to get ahead.

ENVIRONMENT: Editorial and production offices often get short shrift when it comes to space and comfort. In other words, expect little or no privacy and lots of office noise. Sales offices are usually more private and spacious than editorial quarters, although several people may share one office. In circulation, you'll get your own desk and maybe your own VDT, but don't expect a private office until you've reached a more senior level.

WORKSTYLE: In editorial, much of your time will be spent at a desk or in meetings. Most interviewing is done by phone, and everyone, regardless of rank, spends a great deal of time at the typewriter or VDT. In sales, when you're not on the phone making appointments, you'll be making out-of-the-office client calls. In circulation, the day is largely spent at your desk making calls or working with numbers. Count on plenty of meetings. Because production interacts with both editorial and sales departments, you're often in other people's offices, although plenty of time is spent proofreading at your desk.

TRAVEL: In editorial, shelve any dreams you might have of interviews in Hollywood or conferences in Aspen—at least until you're at the level of associate or senior editor or have made your mark as a star writer. There are many more travel opportunities in sales, since you'll go wherever business beckons, which includes trips to trade shows and conferences. If you're a field-based rep, you'll be doing a lot of road travel to cover accounts in your area. Senior people in circulation will occasionally be called on to visit fulfillment houses. In production, there's very little travel, except when you're involved in quality control, working with the production managers to ensure that the printer's work meets quality standards.

EXTRACURRICULAR ACTIVITIES/WORK EXPERIENCE

Campus publications (newspaper, yearbook, alumni publications)—
    reporting, writing, copyediting, doing page layouts, working
    with typesetter, selling space
Society for Collegiate Journalists, Sigma Delta Chi—student member
    ber
Part-time or summer jobs with local newspaper, magazine, or print
    shop
Sales experience of any kind

INTERNSHIPS

The American Society of Magazine Editors (ASME) offers ten-week paid summer internships at consumer and trade magazines in New York, NY, to about 50 students each year. It is open to those between their junior and senior years. Application deadline: December 15. Contact: Robert E. Kenyon, Jr., Executive Director, ASME, 575 Lexington Avenue, New York, NY 10022.

Many magazines take several interns every year, although interns may be hired on an unpaid basis. For more information, write to the editor-in-chief or managing editor of publications that interest you. A good source of internship leads is the *Magazine Publishers of America Summer Internship Program*, 575 Lexington Avenue, New York, NY 10022.

RECOMMENDED READING

BOOKS

The Fanciest Dive: What Happened When the Giant Media Empire of Time-Life Leapt Without Looking into the Age of High Tech, by Christopher Byron, W. W. Norton & Company: 1986

The Great American Magazine: An Inside History of Life, by Loudon Wainwright, Knopf: 1986

Magazines Career Directory, Ron Fry, ed., Career Press Inc.: 1988

MIMP, Magazine Industry Market Place: the Directory of American Periodical Publishing, R. R. Bowker Company (annual)

Opportunities in Magazine Publishing, by John Tebbel, National Textbook Company: 1986

Twenty Years of Rolling Stone, by Jann S. Wenner, Friendly Press: 1987

PERIODICALS

Advertising Age (weekly), Crain Communications, 740 North Rush Street, Chicago, IL 60611

Folio: The Magazine for Magazine Management, Folio Magazine Publishing Co., 6 River Bend, P.O. Box 4949, Stamford, CT 06907-4949

Media Industry Newsletter (weekly), 145 East 49th Street, New York, NY 10017

Magazine & Booksellers (monthly), 401 N. Broad Street, Philadelphia, PA 19108

Magazine Design & Production, Globecom Publishing, Ltd., 4551 West 107th Street, Suite 343, Overland Park, KS 66207

Magazine Week (weekly), Lighthouse Communications, 5 Commonwealth Road, Natick, MA 01760

PROFESSIONAL ASSOCIATION

American Society of Magazine Editors
575 Lexington Avenue
New York, NY 10022

INTERVIEWS

JULIE MCGOWAN
ADVERTISING DIRECTOR
DETAILS MAGAZINE

I became interested in publishing through summer secretarial jobs at two trade publications, *Supermarket News* and *Footwear News*. In addition to learning the basics about magazine publishing, those experiences helped me to decide that I wanted to pursue advertising sales. I didn't feel my talents lay on the editorial side, nor did I want to try to survive on an editorial assistant's salary in New York City. Also, sales is clearly a good path to the top jobs in publishing.

I landed an interview with the president of *Parade Magazine*, who said that he wasn't going to hand me a rate card and send me out on the street with their ad pages commanding $160,000 per page. But he did hire me as a sales trainee with the understanding that I would eventually get my own account list. I spent nine months learning how research, promotion, and production relate to ad sales.

I then moved to Condé Nast and my first position was in the

corporate department. I sold packages of magazines to clients. This was a discount opportunity for large volume advertisers.

This turned out to be a great place because I met all the publicity and advertising directors and sales people. I found myself involved with all the executives at Condé Nast.

After two years at Condé Nast I moved to *Self* magazine. There I had a specific account list, predominantly cosmetics, liquor and tobacco companies. I spent two years there and was eventually promoted to the beauty market manager.

In my current position at *Details*, I decide in conjunction with the publisher how the magazine should be positioned; how to handle circulation; how much money will be allocated for promotion. I no longer have an account list, but I do some selling in conjunction with the sales people.

Being articulate and giving a good presentation are paramount, if you want to be successful in ad space sales. Learn how to listen because you can talk your way past a sale if you're not careful. Information gathering is selling. Clients are not really interested in your magazine but in a marketing solution for their particular product.

As a salesperson your job is to make the link between your magazine and what the client is trying to achieve. Be aggressive, but be careful not to harass. Thoughtfulness and perserverance are the key ingredients.

It can be difficult to break into advertising sales. Trade magazines are an easier place to start than consumer magazines. Also try selling classified ads, that's a way of breaking in and getting experience. Some people also come in from the advertising agency side.

I would say it is not a good idea to start as a sales assistant. On the editorial side the assistant position is an apprenticeship position but in magazine ad sales the assistant position is strictly clerical and not viewed as a jumping off place.

The Radcliffe Publishing Procedures course was good for net-working and meeting people in the industry when I first began. Also Careers for Women in New York City gives a sales course for those who want to break into ad space sales. Any of the seminars given by *MPA* and *Folio Magazine* can be useful as an introduction for learning some of the vocabulary of the business. It's also crucial to read *Ad Week* and *Advertising Age*.

The major hurdle in sales is overcoming the enormous amount of rejection and getting to work the next day. The payoff is that you can make a lot of money along the way since you are compensated on the basis of performance.

TERRI KARUSH
EDITORIAL ASSISTANT
COSMOPOLITAN MAGAZINE
NEW YORK, NY

This is my first year out of college. After graduating from New York University with a degree in journalism, I took an internship at *Esquire* magazine as a fact checker. *Esquire* is owned by Hearst publications, so I became friendly with the people in personnel and landed the job at *Cosmopolitan* magazine.

My duties are varied. The bulk of my time is spent working as the assistant to the executive editor. I am also the poetry editor for the magazine.

The executive editor is only in the office three days a week so when she is out I have time to do some writing and to read the tons of unsolicited poems that are sent to the magazine. I weed out 10 or 20 from the few hundred that I read and send them down to the editor for the final selection.

I spend time opening the mail going through all the press releases and queries from people who want to be in the magazine. Also my typing skills are a plus since the assistant position is generally clerical, although you are using it as a start, and will hopefully move up.

Part of what the executive editor does is assign writers for different projects on the magazine. I'll be working with my first writer. We will go through the ideas-book developed by the editors and decide on the project.

This is a good first job because I am working with the top editors at the magazine. I'm encouraged to read all of the memos so I get to see the inner workings. I can see the reasoning behind the decisions that affect all aspects of the magazine.

I make on the high end of what most assistants make but it is still very low for living in New York City. However, it is a very fluid industry and the skills I develop here can be used in other industries.

One of the best ways to break into the field is as a fact checker. When initially applying for a position mention in your cover letter that you are interested in free lance or full-time work as a fact checker. I got a number of responses to the letters I sent out; the magazines called me. The position pays fairly well and the only qualification you usually need is a college degree.

I chose magazine over book publishing because I like the faster pace here. Although the industry is not as glamourous as I expected, the people are very nice, with almost a family atmosphere.

MEDIA PRODUCTION

The print medium used to be the chief communication tool for corporations, whether to present a new product in an advertising campaign or explain job responsibilities and employment benefits to new employees. With the dawn of the radio age, however, print became only one of a growing number of such tools. Radio and TV advertising complemented, and in many cases replaced, print ads. Direct-mail campaigns were joined by a nonprint counterpart, the telemarketing campaign.

The variety of corporate communication media began growing in earnest in the 1970s, with the advent of the industrial-show concept. The automobile industry was first to experiment with such shows, which typically included the use of audio-visual aids as well as live actors in product presentations to regional dealers and important clients.

Such shows have grown tremendously in popularity and sophistication, to the point that "presentations" is a critical buzzword in corporate communications circles. With the advent of video recording, multi-image projection, computer graphics, and videoconferencing, many corporations have come to rely heavily on audio-visual productions. A-V productions include slide shows with dozens of projectors flashing images and information at a rapid-fire pace, self-contained video productions including live action and computer-generated displays, conferences that link participants at remote sites nationwide or around the world, anything that technology allows. Technology has, in fact, dictated the pace of change in the media production field. A-V producers were using videocassette recorders long before VCRs were available to the general public. Computers built specifically to coordinate multi-image slide shows or generate computer graphics and type were in use before the computer revolution changed the rest of corporate America. For this reason, the ability to understand and use new technology is important for A-V producers.

Career opportunities in the A-V field include the following:

◆ **DESIGN AND PRODUCTION**

◆ **SALES**

◆ **PROGRAMMING**

◆ **VIDEO PRODUCTION**

These areas offer great creative potential for a hard-working person with talent, skill, and a broad base of interest. But a good art background simply isn't enough. Experience in communications, marketing, broadcasting, and technical expertise with computers and video and film equipment are enormously important to the graduate wishing to break into the multimedia field. In addition, a strong liberal arts concentration with a knowledge of many different subject areas is vital when dealing with clients as diversified as chemical manufacturers, stock analysts, and toy companies.

Multi-image slide shows and video or film presentations are generated by three types of producers: independent producers contracted by corporate clients to produce shows, public relations and advertising firms with special media divisions, and in-house media departments in the larger corporations or government agencies. Job possibilities are most abundant in the last category, but the opportunity for real creative work and complex, imaginative, highly budgeted presentations exists primarily in the first two categories. Often the three interrelate: a corporation will use its full-service public relations firm to assist in conceptualizing a large media program, and that firm, in turn, will hire out some of its production to an independent company.

Industrial films, tapes, and slide shows are produced for a variety of purposes—for in-house training and job orientation, to introduce a new product to employees and to the professional community at large, for trade and sales conventions, and to explain benefits packages. Sometimes the chairman of the board or the president of the firm wants to send a message to all the firm's employees around the country, or around the world. A video is the perfect medium for this.

Being an art major is not essential for entering this field, but an ability to see the visual appeal of a product or a campaign and to translate that into promotable, creative material is a high priority. This is an industry in which deadlines are everything, and in which employees can't lose track of the end result, regardless of the hectic pace at which they may have to produce. It goes without saying that neatness counts. When you're working on a series of storyboards that will be turned into slides, you must keep the bigger picture in mind. When those renderings are magnified 40-fold in front of a camera, any flaw will ruin the whole effect.

A creative approach to problem solving, flexibility, and technical knowledge of how to get the job done are necessary for a career as a designer or producer. A knowledge of the A-V field as well as of your particular client's field, an assertive manner, and an unwillingness to take no for an answer are essential if you're interested in a career in A-V sales. Vast expertise in computer typography and graphics, good timing, accuracy, speed, a knowledge of film and video editing, and the ability to work long hours on small details without tiring are vital if you want to become an A-V programmer. Experience in film and video editing and an awareness of what the medium can and can't do is important if you're interested in becoming a video producer. Just because you begin in one specialty, doesn't necessarily mean you'll end up there. Because the field of audio-visual production is so new, there are a lot of career musical chairs. A board artist can become an account executive; a good A-V technician may become a programmer or a producer.

JOB OUTLOOK

JOB OPENINGS WILL GROW: About as fast as average

COMPETITION FOR JOBS: Strong

Although audio-visual production for industrial and corporate presentations has grown tremendously, it is still a small field compared with well-established business segments like advertising and commercial film production. Although most companies in the Fortune 500 now have some sort of media production department, or a public relations or marketing department with media facilities, most such departments are small. While the number of independent media production houses is also growing, those companies are also typically on the small side.

NEW JOB OPPORTUNITIES: As corporations look to trim their operating budgets and increase the productivity of their work forces, established ways of doing business are coming under close scrutiny and in some instances are falling by the wayside. Travel costs are the third-largest controllable expense in the average corporation's budget; corporations now spend over $100 billion per year on travel and entertainment. One way to keep a lid on travel costs, many companies have found, is to use video technology. With videoconferencing, companies can set up conference rooms at various branch offices nationwide or even worldwide, and connect those rooms via satellite, microwave, or telecommunications transmission. This allows participants in the various rooms to communicate with one another "over the air," as if they were sitting in the same room.

Improvements in technology that are expected in the near future will make videoconferencing a more affordable and more useful alternative to in-person meetings. Computer systems already exist that enable videoconferences to take place on a computer screen. With these systems, not only do participants see and hear one another, but they can also exchange computer data and display presentation graphics on the screens of all participants. Videoconferencing clearly will be a major force in media production as we roll into the 21st century.

GEOGRAPHIC JOB INDEX

Large corporations with A-V or media capabilities can be found all over the country. However, the plum jobs with independent producers and public relations firms are generally in the biggest cities, particularly New York, NY, and Los Angeles, CA. If you start out in the media production department of an oil company or a life insurance firm in a small city, you may eventually have to look for your next job in New York if you want to move up.

WHO THE EMPLOYERS ARE

CORPORATIONS that have substantial media departments include AT&T, Avon Products, Equitable Life Assurance, Exxon, General Foods, IBM, Merrill Lynch, Metropolitan Life Insurance, Rockwell International, Texaco, Travelers, and Union Carbide, to name a few. You can try their main headquarters, as well as their branch offices and divisions around the country.

THE UNITED STATES GOVERNMENT has many divisions, from the United States Information Agency to the armed forces, that create their own training films. Three years ago, the government had enough A-V staff, equipment and presentation space to fill the Empire State Building two and half times over! There are 30,000 to 50,000 A-V positions within the government structure. All of these jobs, however, are located in the Washington, DC, area. You can contact the National Audio-Visual Center in Capitol Heights, MD, for information on government opportunities in this area.

NONPROFIT AND OTHER GOVERNMENT MARKETS employ many A-V people. State and local governments around the country have such jobs, generally through their PR departments. Community and religious agencies have a certain number of low-paying positions available, as do schools and universities. Scientific and public health information organizations are also potential employers.

PUBLIC RELATIONS AND ADVERTISING FIRMS rarely have their own media departments. Most contract with independent producers for their clients' needs, but the largest employ their own producer and a small staff. You can try calling any one of the Fortune 500 companies and ask who handles the PR and ad accounts. Then you can call the firms themselves (nearly all of them will be in New York, NY, or Los Angeles, CA) and inquire about career possibilities there. Generally, the firms that do have their own A-V departments require at least a year of experience in corporate A-V or independent production.

INDEPENDENT PRODUCTION COMPANIES are the source of the most exciting and creative jobs. Some of these companies are just a couple of people in a studio who free lance out most of their production work. Some have considerable facilities of their own, including an entire art department, special effects cameras, screening rooms with multiple projectors, a sound department, and a substantial sales staff.

If you start with a small outfit, you have a greater possibility of having hands-on participation in every aspect of the business. On the other hand, the clients will be small, the budgets for shows minimal, and your clients won't grow as quickly. Most of the independent production companies are in large cities: New York, NY, Los Angeles, CA, Chicago, IL, Dallas, TX, Detroit, MI, Orlando, FL, and the area around Washington, DC, Baltimore,

MD, and Richmond, VA. The National Audio-Visual Association, 3150 Spring Street, Fairfax, VA 22031, can provide a listing of most of the independent producers around the country.

HOW TO BREAK INTO THE FIELD

Because the audio-visual field is such an eclectic one, you're going to have to use your ingenuity to find a job. If you know someone already in the industry, use any contacts or referrals he or she can give you. You may never see an ad in the help-wanted section of the newspaper for a position in this field, and therefore it's important to be a self-starter and go after the job you really want. If you do see an offering for a secretary or receptionist at an independent producer's office, apply for it, by all means! It is most common in this field for people to be promoted from within, so don't be afraid of starting at the bottom.

Once you have some names of producers and corporations with large A-V departments, you should compose a letter of introduction to send along with your résumé. This letter should state your academic background, your specific interests, and any experience you've had with computers or A-V equipment. Write to the head of the department you're interested in—the sales manager, the production manager, the head designer, etc. Follow up your letter with a phone call, and try to line up an interview. You should become familiar with the specific work of an independent producer and know who its primary clients are; when approaching a corporation, you should familiarze yourself with the A-V needs of its various departments.

One of the best ways to start out in this field is free lancing. Many of today's top A-V people began working for companies on an hourly basis while they were still in art school or college. Very often, a small company doesn't really need a full staff of artists or production people and will hire out work whenever it is really busy. But free lancing can be a great deal more than just getting a foot in the door. Often, a really talented designer or programmer develops a following, and clients will ask for him or her specifically when a project comes up. Some of the most important corporate jobs are farmed out to specialists, who can earn top dollar. If you're a self-disciplined person who can always be trusted to get the job done on time and don't mind hustling for work, free lancing may be the way to create a career for yourself in multimedia. On the other hand, if you prefer the organized setting of an office, with a regular salary and all the other inherent benefits, you may be able to land a good staff position by starting with a firm as a free lancer.

Whether you are applying for a full-time job or a free lance assignment, be sure you have your portfolio up-to-date. The artwork you present may have nothing to do with the ultimate A-V production you eventually get involved with, but your samples will show what you can do. Multimedia productions require many hands working on many aspects of the presentation. You should be able to demonstrate that you can do a variety of things—graphic design, cartooning, photography, and color work are just a few examples. All your work should have flair and originality. By all means be certain that every selection in your portfolio is neat, accurate, and displayed to its best advantage.

INTERNATIONAL JOB OPPORTUNITIES

Although a great deal of audio-visual work is now being done in Europe and Japan, it's very difficult to break into this field abroad, particularly because a knowledge of specific national corporations and their special industrial needs is necessary. Unless you're fluent in the language of the country where you wish to be employed, you'll have no hope whatsoever of finding a job there.

However, many American companies now have offices abroad. If you work your way up in the field, you may find yourself taking an occasional transatlantic trip to oversee an A-V production or a video or film that requires a foreign location. Also, many American companies hold their sales conferences in lush, exotic locations. If you're the producer or programmer of such a corporate event, you may take your show on the road outside the United States.

ENTREPRENEURIAL

Videocassette recorders certainly have altered the way Americans spend their leisure hours. They are also changing the way many corporations perform some critical functions—most notably, how they train their employees to do new jobs.

Small businesses usually don't have the resources to hire full-time trainers or contract with outside services for teachers and trainers for their office personnel. But books and documentation usually aren't enough to make employees comfortable with new tasks, particularly if those tasks involve the use of technology. Enter video-based training. A number of independent producers, among them comedic actor John Cleese, have created successful enterprises that make and sell video-based training programs to businesses.

Of course, knowledge of video production is but one element in a successful video-based training venture. Equally important is having a strong and detailed knowledge of the training subject. Many independent training ventures have both a technical expert and a consultant that specializes in employee training.

The costs of developing and producing a video-based training series can be high, but not out of reach. For instance, to get funding or to make those big sales, some independent producers have been able to work deals with third parties, sellers of computer equipment or software.

DESIGN AND PRODUCTION

The designer or producer assists the clients in conceptualizing a media presentation that will best solve the creative problem at hand. If the client is the company management, and they want an effective tool to explain the past year's progress at their annual meeting, the producer must devise a program—be it live action, multi-image slides, video, film, or a combination of these, to get that message across. The producer also has to learn to work creatively within a budget and to give the client the most for his or her money.

In a very large firm, there will be both a designer, who is responsible for the visualization and graphic execution of an idea, and a producer, who coordinates all the departments—sound, photography, art, etc. In smaller firms, these two functions are combined in one job.

The production department consists of board artists, who execute the storyboard for the show according to the designer's specifications and do any other artwork necessary, such as a flip-chart that might be used at a meeting; slide mounters, who mount the negatives, clean them, check them for errors and organize them; special effects photographers, who shoot the slides or film; and production assistants, who work directly for the designer or producer. A variety of free lance specialists, such as a script writer, a camera crew, or a top designer, may also be involved.

The production department works closely with the sound engineers, who produce the soundtrack for the show, a combination of narration and music. The audio and video must be mixed by the programmer. Many independent companies have their own sound departments, but some hire out to free lance units.

QUALIFICATIONS

PERSONAL: A capacity to complete long, sometimes tedious work. Ability to take directions, but also the creative impulse to devise unusual solutions to problems. A sense of tact. Ability to handle pressure and tight deadlines.

PROFESSIONAL: Artistic talent, imagination, accuracy, neatness. Knowledge of the limitations and potential of a variety of technical equipment.

CAREER PATHS

LEVEL	JOB TITLE	EXPERIENCE NEEDED
Entry	Production assistant	College degree or art school
2	Board artist, photographer	Art school or 1–2 years

| 3 | Head photographer, associate producer | 3–5 years (associate producer needs computer skills) |
| 4 | Designer/producer | 5–10 years (computer and video skills needed) |

JOB RESPONSIBILITIES ♦ ENTRY LEVEL

PRODUCTION ASSISTANT
THE BASICS: Assisting producer, running errands, scouting halls for setup of multi-image shows, booking hotels for live talent.

MORE CHALLENGING DUTIES: Assembling slides according to written script and numbering them. Putting slides in sleeves according to category. Coordinating art and photography departments' schedules. Maintaining slide files.

BOARD ARTIST
THE BASICS: Executing designs according to producer's specifications. Assembling storyboards. Doing paste-ups. Drawing charts and graphs.

MORE CHALLENGING DUTIES: Taking over for producer. Supervising other artists. Carrying small jobs through from start to finish.

MOVING UP

A production assistant has a great deal of opportunity to move up in an organization, as does a board artist. If you've been working diligently for a year in an independent company, you may be asked to accompany your boss to conventions, sales conferences, or to participate in a client's annual meeting. As you make contacts with people outside your immediate firm, you can become more and more visible, which is enormously important for a successful multimedia person. As clients get to know you and realize that they can rely on you, you have more of a chance to make an impression. A client may very likely ask for you to participate in future projects. A number of such requests can put you in line for a promotion to assistant or associate producer within your own company. You may also be able to meet people in larger companies or corporations who may be hiring at the next level up. In either case, your chief asset is your ability to work well with people under pressure.

SALES

A sales rep or account executive (found only in the independent production companies) sells a particular client on his or her company's product—a multi-image show, a video or film. If you're not a shrinking violet and enjoy convincing people, the rewards of a sales position can be very great indeed. It will be your job to scout out the various local and national companies, learn what their particular problems are, understand their perspective on their product, and persuade them that you can create a media campaign that will increase their business or make their corporation a better place for its employees to work. It's important to be aggressive, but you must also keep up-to-date files and always follow up on the many phone calls you make. Once you have sparked a client's interest, it's vital that you show the client exactly what your company can do—by inviting him or her to see your facility and other productions you've mounted. Persistence and ambition are the only way to the top in A-V sales.

Your job is not always an easy one, because your company may be in competition with the client's own A-V department or PR firm. You'll only gain accounts by convincing the client that you, as an independent producer, offer the most complete and professional services.

QUALIFICATIONS

PERSONAL: An outgoing personality. Great powers of persuasion. Energy, drive, and persistence.

PROFESSIONAL: Knowledge of your field and its technical capabilities. Ability to get interested in your client's field. Good organizational skills. General knowledge of marketing. For entry-level positions, good typing skills (45 words per minute or better) and pleasant phone manner.

CAREER PATHS

LEVEL	JOB TITLE	EXPERIENCE NEEDED
Entry	Sales assistant	College degree
2	Sales representative/account executive	1–2 years
3	Sales manager	4–10 years

JOB RESPONSIBILITIES ◆ ENTRY LEVEL

THE BASICS: Answering phones. Typing letters, photocopying, and filing. Light computer work, e.g., typing into a terminal and entering account information.

MORE CHALLENGING DUTIES: Accompanying account executives on sales calls. Handling a few small accounts with supervision. Researching possible new accounts by writing letters and making phone calls.

MOVING UP

As an account executive, it will be your responsibility to generate new accounts and maintain old ones. The major users of audiovisual presentations are the large corporations, but the small ones can't be overlooked. Most sales departments have thick resource books that list companies locally and nationally, and give the names of their presidents or chief executive officers. By contacting clients and interesting them in your product, you'll develop a following. The company that commissions a training film today may need a multi-image slide show for its annual meeting tomorrow. If you can persuade a potential new account to take a look at your firm's past productions, you may be able to convince the new account to give your company all its A-V business.

It will also be important for you to act as a liaison between your production department and the client's PR department. You may have to supervise younger sales representatives and oversee some of their more difficult accounts. It may be your responsibility to travel to the various sales conferences or conventions at which your product appears.

If you develop a strong following and have a long record of sales success, you may eventually become head of your department, or sales manager. The manager sets and implements sales policy and trains the incoming staff.

PROGRAMMING

Programming a complex A-V production is a difficult job and requires a sort of Renaissance person with vast knowledge and expertise in many different areas. The programmer's job is similar to that of a stage manager or a director of a theatrical production, it's his or her responsibility to see that everything fits together smoothly and runs like clockwork. This means hands-on performance with computers, projectors, audio equipment, cameras, and video recorders, as well as an ability to meld many different workers into an effective team that functions as one organism.

QUALIFICATIONS

PERSONAL: Leadership ability, perfectionism, organizational skills, foresight. Ability to work well under pressure and to work well with others.

PROFESSIONAL: Enormous technical knowledge; expertise with a variety of machines. Good timing, ability to do difficult detail work quickly and accurately.

CAREER PATHS

LEVEL	JOB TITLE	EXPERIENCE NEEDED
Entry	Word processor/computer typographer, A-V technician	High school
2	Programming assistant	1–2 years
3	Video/film/slide editor	2–4 years
4	Programmer	5–10 years

JOB RESPONSIBILITIES ♦ ENTRY LEVEL

THE BASICS: Placing type selections in computer; running machine. Assisting programmer to follow the script and the organized slide sleeves and to program the computer that will run multiple projectors.

MORE CHALLENGING DUTIES: Doing basic film or video editing. Pulsing a tape recorder to run a simple two-projector show. Accompanying programmer to setup and performance of multi-image show.

MOVING UP

Many paths may lead to the coveted position of programmer. Some people start as A-V technicians and come up through the corporate video ranks (see below). With sufficient technical expertise, a computer typographer or projectionist can work up to becoming video services coordinator—someone who writes and edits tapes and produces them for his or her company. With this kind of experience, it's easier to land a programming job in an independent firm, where the variety of work is greater and the opportunities, therefore, are unlimited. A programmer may work with videotape, videodisc, or film; he or she may be responsible for shows that involve still slides, overheads, opaques, or filmstrips. A programmer may also direct video or film transfers of multi-image shows.

Everyone depends on the programmer. Without him or her, nothing would fit together and, consequently, there would be no show. For this reason, you must be completely dependable and enormously talented to move up in the programming field. But if you're good and develop a following, you can go anywhere and name your price. The possibilities are vast for a successful programmer.

VIDEO PRODUCTION

Video production may be handled by the design and production people, but it deserves a mention on its own, because it may be a separate department in an independent production company, and in the corporate world it may be the whole in-house A-V department. The video producer must have a similar background to that of the A-V designer and the programmer, with a concentration in video and film. Of course, the video producer must know how to edit film, how to work with live actors, and how to manage a budget.

The head of most corporate media departments is most often a video producer, because the majority of in-house A-V presentations are self-contained videos. You can make a video for about one-third the cost of a film and for about one-half the cost of a multimedia image show, hence the in-house preference for videos.

ADDITIONAL INFORMATION

SALARIES

Production assistants and A-V technicians generally earn in the mid-teens to low-twenties annually. Board artists get about $15 to $20 an hour. Photographers with art school degrees can begin at about $20,000 a year, as can someone trained in computer graphics. The field can be fairly lucrative, however. A top designer on staff can earn $40,000 to $50,000 a year.

In programming, the entry-level positions are poorly paid, a starting salary might be $16,000 a year or less. However, an experienced programmer may earn $50,000 and up per year; the career opportunities are considerable.

WORKING CONDITIONS

HOURS: As in any situation in which there are tight deadlines, hours can be long and erratic. In a PR firm, clients are billed for their time, which makes it imperative for all departments to operate on an efficient schedule. The days (and nights) just before a multimedia show or a film shoot are generally the most hectic in any A-V company, and even the production assistants may be expected to put in extra time without pay. Entry-level sales and computer people usually work from nine to five, but that changes as they work their way up in the ranks.

In an independent production company, hours are much looser than in a corporation or in a PR or advertising agency. As long as you get your job done and are available for scheduled meetings, nobody will clock you in and out. In a corporation, however, structure is everything. There are set hours, and deviation from the routine is frowned on. You must take this into account when considering where you might best fit in.

Multimedia shows tend to take place at year-end conventions or in the spring, when a company rewards its employees for good work done the previous year with a trip to an exotic locale. This means that December, January, and February are busiest in independent production houses as the staff works furiously to accommodate clients. Video and film production is not usually seasonal, which means that the workload for in-house A-V departments is generally spread evenly throughout the year.

ENVIRONMENT: Work environments vary widely in the A-V field. In an independent production company or small media studio, your "office" may be little more than a corner of a room with a desk. In a corporate environment you may work under the same conditions as any other member of that company in any other department, the higher you go, the larger your office. If you're a technical person, you will probably spend most of your time surrounded by equipment of one sort or another.

Because the production end of the job involves setups in different locations, you may find yourself in hotel convention halls or out in the field, filming or doing still camera work. If you're in the sales department, you may have to spend a good part of your day traveling around the city, visiting clients.

People in independent companies tend to dress casually, and it's not uncommon to see an entire production staff in jeans and T-shirts. In a corporate environment, however, dress in the A-V department may be as formal as that required in any division of a Fortune 500 company.

The feeling in most multimedia departments is one of immediacy, and there's little time to sit back and relax. Phones ring constantly and people rush around from one department to another in this hectic, fast-moving atmosphere.

WORKSTYLE: Production people must learn to work anywhere— sitting at a desk producing and organizing slides, running around setting up shoots, or dealing with free lance camera and sound crews in their own studios.

Salespeople spend a good deal of time on the telephone, showing clients the company's facilities, and visiting the clients' offices. They may frequently conduct business over lunch.

Programmers spend most of their time in front of editing machines or computers. They also travel to the various shows to supervise the presentations.

TRAVEL: Opportunities for travel increase as you work your way up in the A-V field, and the heads of production and programming departments may be asked to make occasional trips across the country or across the ocean for important conventions or meetings.

Free lance designers and programmers travel even more frequently, because they must go wherever the particular client is.

Less traveling is involved, of course, if you work in-house on training films and presentations, but even in this situation it may be necessary to visit different locations and appear at sales conferences.

EXTRACURRICULAR ACTIVITIES/WORK EXPERIENCE

Student theatrical productions—working lights and/or sound equipment, creating publicity brochures or posters, ticket sales
Audio-visual aide for campus films and lectures
Photographer for campus events
Part-time or summer employment in sales

INTERNSHIPS

No internships, as such, are offered by the A-V industry. A first job at a small independent production company, however, is tantamount to an internship, because it involves training in every aspect of the business. Several of the industry associations, such as the National Audio-Visual Association and the Society of Motion Picture and Television Engineers hold annual conferences and offer seminars and training at these meetings.

RECOMMENDED READING

BOOKS

AV Market Place (1989): The Complete Business Directory of: Audio, Audio-Visual, Film, Video, Programming, R. R. Bowkers Database Publishing Group: 1989

Career Opportunities in Television, Cable and Video, by Maxine K. and Robert M. Reed: 1986

PERIODICALS

Audio-visual Communications, PTN Publishing, 210 Crossway Park Drive, Woodbury, NY 11797

A-V Video, Montage Publishing Inc., 25550 Hawthorne Blvd., Ste. 314 Torrance, CA 90505

Technical Photography, PTN Publishing, 210 Crossway Park Drive, Woodbury, NY 11797

PROFESSIONAL ASSOCIATIONS

Association for Multi-Imaging (AMI)
8019 North Himes Avenue, Ste. 401
Tampa, FL 33614

ITVA (International Television Associates)
6311 North O'Connor Road
Ste 110
Irving, TX 75039

National Audio-Visual Association
8661 Leesburg Pike
Tysons Park, VA 22180

National Audio-Visual Center
8700 Edgeworth Drive
Capital Heights, MD 20743

Society of Motion Picture and Television Engineers (SMPTE)
595 West Hartsdale Avenue
White Plains, NY 10607

INTERVIEWS

JAMES A. BRADY
MANAGER OF MEDIA PRODUCTION SERVICES
UNION CARBIDE CORPORATION
DANBURY, CT

I was always interested in media—I remember when I was 13, running around school grabbing up all the slide projectors to do my own version of the Joshua Light show for the midwinter dance! I belonged to the radio and electronics clubs, anything to get into the field. If they'd had videotape in those days, I would have taped the school football games.

I went to a state university in New York and majored in broadcasting with a minor in education. The educational curriculum—what we called "lick 'em, stick 'em"—was the only channel in those days for getting any audio-visual experience. We had to learn how to make flash cards, how to do color graphics and heat-seal them on cardboard for presentations. I learned color-slide E4 processing in the bathroom sink!

I got my first job at Union Carbide in 1976 as an A-V production assistant. That meant I did a lot of moving chairs around for meetings and setting up projectors. Sometimes I'd get involved in programming, but it was a long while before I was really producing a show. In our corporation, we mostly do video for training and product promotion, and I found that my best route up the ladder was learning as much as I could about video and film production.

We rarely do big slide shows—the multi-image presentations that make such a splash at huge conventions—partly because of the expense involved, but mostly because video makes communication so much more accessible. You don't have to gather all your hundreds of employees in one place to explain a benefits package to them. You can produce one tape and send copies around the country.

I think it's important for anyone with an art background to get as much film and video experience as possible. They have to understand idea sequence to get their storyboard right, and they have to know the new technology of the field to be able to design for it. Also, they've got to learn to keyboard a computer. Artwork in multimedia isn't done with pens and paper anymore—a Genagraphics machine makes slides directly on the computer; a Dubner machine does video animation. Based on my own experience, I think anyone starting out today should get as diversified a background as possible. That way, he or she will be prepared to go into any number of the new media areas.

PETER DOUGLAS
PRODUCER
VINCENT PICTURES
UNIVERSAL STUDIOS
UNIVERSAL CITY, CA

I had a lot of different ideas about what I wanted to do. During college I wanted to do photography. I was supplementing my income by working in production over one summer and I found myself more attracted to production than taking pictures. First, I entered the Director's Guild Training Program. This is a really hard program to get into, particularly these days, because there is such a demand for it. But they do take a few people after a series of interviews and tests. The program sets you up as a "second assistant director trainee." There is a certain time requirement before you become a full fledged "second." Then there are certain time requirements before you become a full fledged "first." And, I believe, an additional time requirement to be a production manager. This is the process to become a set manager who makes sure that all the production elements are on the set each day at the correct time, anticipates delays and needs and works with budgets.

I focus more on the creative side than on the production side, so my days are different than other producers'. For one thing, I write a lot. I spend most of my day looking at materials to develop—whether it's the actual script or stories that I can get someone else to carry a little further. You're spending most of your time getting the origins of a film together, which is a script. You can also set up a development deal to develop that script, but that is more difficult because development funds are very difficult to come by. There is a high risk element here. I don't know what the odds are, but I wouldn't be surprised if for every one picture that gets made there are 250 scripts that don't.

To develop a script you have to hire a writer to develop an idea or advance a script. Then you have to find a director who will direct it. And, of course, you have to find financing and cast the movie.

Then you have to put all these things together. I mean this is an oversimplification, but that's basically what you do.

The most important thing you should know if you want to go into the production business is that it is not a production business. It's distribution. The media business today is a business of marketing. So, the most important attribute you ought to have is the power to make relationships. You should have a personality that attracts people. You should also be able to deal with large egos. That is part of the process.

If you are interested in the motion picture business I would suggest that you definitely pursue your education, particularly your reading skills, because traditionally you start as a reader for somebody. You can't possibly read everything that you get, so you hire people who try to comb out a germ of something that might interest you. So you share scripts with people that you trust and have the ability to convey what they have read. Then you look at some short form synopses. The most important skill at the start is typing and shorthand. When I am looking for assistants and evaluating which is the best bet, short of formal film school training, these skills are a major, major attribute.

The careers in the movie industry fragment quite a bit, much like in the medical profession. If you want to be a producer, there are a number of ways to break into the business. You have to have a contact to start with who can find out where there are openings. I don't mean to make this sound simple at all, finding these jobs is very tough—they are in very big demand. I can't tell you how many students come to me looking for work for the summer. Most of the time I just don't have anything for them.

There are other avenues. A lot of the top theatrical agencies have training programs. Maybe you could start in the mail room of the studio. I guarantee you this will come in handy. I don't think sending out a mass of computer generated letters to people is very helpful. You want to get in, on the inside. And the way you do that is to apply for jobs in the mail room and other go-fer jobs that pay very little. But you have to get on the inside, that's the first step. If you have a contact, use him. On occasion I do hear that someone is looking for a job and I hear someone is interviewing and I can put them together. That is the best of all worlds.

Beyond this there is also the Director Guild's Training Program. Another avenue is to write your first script and if it's a particularly great script, you're a writer. None of the big agencies are going to bother with you at the start. You need to find a young producer who has a leg up in the business. You shouldn't come out with your first script and expect Steven Spielberg to read it, because it ain't gonna happen. But there are ways—you can find a small agency. They are all listed in the Writer's Guild, and they are listed as to whether they will accept unsolicited material or not. Here too, personal contacts are important—personal contacts are the essence of this business.

In general develop those skills I talked about, speed reading, typing and shorthand, because those are the jobs that are most available to college educated people. The education, by the way, does mean something in getting your first job but it doesn't mean much beyond that. There really is no proper education for the motion picture industry, with the possible exception of one or two film schools who teach you more about the technical side of the film industry. Also, structure yourself in a way that will allow you to pursue a film career. The reason that there are such fantastic up sides in this business is because the down sides are so great. Pursue your specialty and be prepared for rejection. This is a business of rejection—you have to be able to swallow rejection. I have somewhat established myself and I get rejected everyday. You don't take it personally—you just keep working at it. Your basic skills and your intellect are your best asset. You have to come into this business expecting nothing, but if you have the skills, you can get work. The various guilds will help you, so get in touch with them. (And read a book that's been long out of print called the *5 C's of Cinematography* by Joseph Mascelli. You can probably find it in a library somewhere.)

PHIL KRUENER
PRODUCER
REUNION PRODUCTIONS
WATERTOWN, MA

How I got started as a producer was mostly just luck of the draw. I was a religion and philosophy major at a midwestern college and came to Boston to go to graduate school at Harvard. I spent a year at the Divinity School there and dropped out. I was working in a video rental store and I happened to meet a young woman. We became friendly and after about three months she asked me what I really wanted to do. I said that I loved movies and the notion of film making and that I would like to go into some aspect of the business. Well, it turns out that her father was a producer in Boston and she gave me his number. I got up my nerve and gave him a call and he told me to come in. We seemed to hit it off. He didn't really have any openings for me at that point, but he told me to give him a call in the next four to six weeks because he was going to begin to work on a documentary on American cities. I followed that up and started going in one day a week as an intern doing general research activities. I wasn't doing anything too interesting or significant. My main duty was to call the Chamber of Commerce of cities we were going to shoot in to find out whether there were any major events happening in the cities. The show was about the rebirth of downtown cities.

What happened, though, was that they started needing old archival film footage. I had always been interested in that kind of thing so they sent me down to Washington to do some basic research. At about the same time I started going on shoots with them. From this I became an assistant editor, and began my association with Reunion Productions. I then went free lance for a couple of months. That was hard because I was bartending to make extra money. I had to make a lot of cold calls to work as a production assistant or as an assistant editor. I guess I impressed Reunion because in January of 1987 they asked me to come back.

We are a production company, not a production house, so we

don't own the equipment. We don't own the cameras or the lights; we don't have editing facilities. We write, produce and direct video tapes primarily for corporations. We also do some broadcast work, primarily because my boss has a long time association with certain channels. My normal day involves a lot of phone calls as well as a lot of creative time—writing proposals and scripts. I have to coordinate people and the locations. I have to get the camera people and the production people and the equipment all working together. I have a lot of client contact, working out exactly what it is they want. We pride ourselves on exploring and understanding fully the needs of the client, even to the point of disagreeing with the client about what their needs are. It's a lot of organizing and managing as well as doing the creative stuff.

What I like most about my job is that we go into different environments. Each production presents a problem with different locations, different people, different styles. Sometimes we need to do a documentary, other times we need to do something dramatic. You have to learn about a lot of different topics to get to the point where you understand what the client is communicating, and what points they are trying to make. On the other hand, the business is very competitive. The hours are long. And the frustrating thing about being a producer is that there is always one detail that you forget, no matter how prepared you are. There is always one thing that you didn't fully get together. This is also the fun part of the business because you have to ad lib.

To break into the film business you should make a lot of phone calls to production companies. There are low-paying, ground-level jobs, and there are higher-end people who make pretty substantial money. You have to be willing to do the lower-end work. In fact, to move up in the film production industry you have to be prepared to do everything and anything you can for no money. Also meet as many people as you can. I think the hardest thing to understand about the business is that it looks so easy, but it actually takes a great deal of time. Keep your money expectations down, because in the beginning you will make less than you'd expect to make in other fields.

I think that there are a lot of opportunities at local cable television stations to get basic experience. I came in with virtually no production experience. I had taken a couple of film history courses in college and watched a lot of old movies, but I regret not having taken more production oriented courses. If you are lucky enough to know that you know that you want to go into film production, acquire those skills before you go out into the market place. If you are out of school, go to your local cable station and volunteer to work in their production facilities. This gives you a good chance to do a lot of hands on work. You can also call production studios, like I did, and go in for an information interview. The film community is generally friendly and helpful, particularly in New England. It may be more uncongenial in other parts of the country, but a lot of people are willing to talk to you and help you get started. If you are really interested in the process of film making, doing things from start to finish (write, produce, shoot, direct, edit), corporate or industrial productions is probably the best way to start. Very few people go right into feature films—you have to be incredibly lucky—but you get good training in industrial film making.

ART MUSEUMS

Certain museum names shine with a luster that reaches around the globe: the Metropolitan Museum of Art, the Guggenheim, the Art Institute of Chicago, the Museum of Modern Art, the J. Paul Getty Museum, the National Gallery of Art, and so on. The big-name museums in major cities aren't the only ones that house notable collections. The art student and art historian interested in museum work can find exciting openings almost anywhere in the United States.

A number of factors have come together in the past decade or so to make museums a more dynamic part of America's cultural scene. One agent of change has been the coming of age of the baby-boom generation, a good proportion of which is college-educated. Museum attendance has increased steadily since the 1970s. In turn, many museums—particularly the larger ones—are aggressively pursuing public support in a variety of ways, from advertising campaigns to product marketing to sponsorship of major touring collections. In recent years, Andrew Wyeth, Pablo Picasso, and Vincent Van Gogh have all gone "on the road," playing, as it were, in dozens of cities to standing-room-only crowds.

Although some critics insist that some museums have gone too far in commercializing the works of the masters, the sad fact is that without a more aggressive tack, many museums could face devastating financial shortfalls. Federal funding, which seemed so plentiful in the 1960s, slowed to a trickle in the 1980s, and the prospects for a return to a more healthful flow are not good. It is, in fact, remarkable that art museums have flourished despite the stinginess of Uncle Sam.

Although the larger metropolitan museums have garnered the lion's share of attention and resources in this museum renaissance, smaller regional museums—some tucked in seemingly out-of-the-way places—have thrived as well. The Sterling and Francine Clark Art Institute, nestled in the northwest corner of Massachusetts on the campus of Williams College, boasts an impressive collection of Impressionist paintings among its holdings. Historic Williamsburg, VA, is home to the Abby Aldrich Rockefeller Folk Art Center and its collection of American folk art pieces.

Although landing a first job at a major museum may appear to be more glamorous, there are advantages to starting out at a smaller museum. The art major entering the field via a smaller institution has a much better opportunity to sample all the various options of museum work, from fund-raising to research to shop sales to special exhibit planning. This kind of well-rounded background can be invaluable in moving on to your ultimate goal.

Competition for curatorial and educational jobs is particularly fierce, but other departments have more accessible entry-level opportunities that may offer similar or even greater satisfaction. There is a particular need for professionals in the administrative and revenue-producing areas.

Technology is finding a place alongside the museum's artifacts of the past. Computers and word processors handle cataloging and bookkeeping, making the clerical work that is so much a part of entry-level jobs less tedious and more efficient. Scholarly catalogs are now written on word processors. Therefore, if you can bring some computer skills to the job, you're likely to be a more attractive applicant.

Entry-level jobs in museums require a college degree, with a major or strong minor in art history. Demonstrated interest in the field, such as internships or volunteer work, will also help you land a position at a museum and, more importantly, will bring you in contact with people who may be helpful in your job search. For curatorial positions, school art history papers are evidence of your research skills and your scholarship. The museum community is an international one, and research sources are often found in their original language. Fluency in another language, therefore, is a definite advantage. For any entry-level job, in any functional area, good typing and clerical skills are essential.

Your first job in a museum, whether you have a B.A., M.A., or even a Ph.D., will be in a support position. In a small museum, you may find yourself setting up chairs for a board meeting one day and double-checking budget figures the next. In a large museum, you would work primarily in one department. Wherever you enter, you will have an opportunity to learn how a museum operates and to explore the area that interests you most. Each career path stresses different skills and attracts people with different aspirations and inclinations; the common characteristic is a passionate interest in art and a solid belief that art should be shared with the public. The major functional areas are:

◆ ADMINISTRATION

◆ CURATORIAL

In addition, entry-level opportunities exist in other departments: the registrar (inventories museum holdings), development (fund raising), education (classes, tours, lectures), publications, public relations (or public information), and sales (museum shops). These jobs allow you to work within the institution, but do not require the advanced education that almost inevitably accompanies the more traditional career paths.

Conservation is yet another option, but only for those graduates with an exceptional dedication to the preservation of art and a willingness to work and study to perfect their skills. No one should consider a career as a conservator without fully investigating this demanding profession.

JOB OUTLOOK

JOB OPENINGS WILL GROW: As fast as average

COMPETITION FOR JOBS: Keen

NEW JOB OPPORTUNITIES: With decreased federal funding for the arts, museums are seeking new ways to support themselves; they are hiring professional grant writers, producing educational programs with which they hope to stimulate greater private interest, and developing retail and mail order sales of museum-inspired gifts as a lucrative source of income. These growing areas offer excellent opportunities, especially at the entry level. Candidates with degrees in arts administration (many of which are offered at the graduate level) are increasingly in demand.

GEOGRAPHIC JOB INDEX

The best-known museums are found in large metropolitan areas. The greatest concentration is in the East, although Texas and California have recently become major museum centers. Many smaller cities support their own museums or historical societies. The American Association of Museums publishes an annual directory listing all accredited museums in the country. Check your library to locate the museums in your area.

WHO THE EMPLOYERS ARE

LARGE MUSEUMS have the most extensive, most highly professional staffs and the most attractive research facilities. Consequently, they are excellent places in which to learn—and highly competitive places in which to find employment.

SMALL MUSEUMS AND LOCAL HISTORICAL SOCIETIES may be a better bet for entry-level jobs. They don't pay as well as large institutions, but because they are often understaffed, you have a better chance of moving up quickly into more responsible positions.

MAJOR EMPLOYERS

Art Institute of Chicago, Chicago, IL
Brooklyn Museum, Brooklyn, NY
Carnegie Institute, Pittsburgh, PA
Cincinnati Art Museum, Cincinnati, OH
Cleveland Museum of Art, Cleveland, OH
Dallas Museum of Fine Arts, Dallas, TX
Detroit Institute of Arts, Detroit, MI
Fine Arts Museum of San Francisco, San Francisco, CA
Gilcrease Institute, Tulsa, OK
J. Paul Getty Museum, Malibu, CA
Los Angeles County Museum, Los Angeles, CA
Metropolitan Museum of Art, New York, NY
Minneapolis Museum of Art, Minneapolis, MN
Museum of American Folk Art, New York, NY
Museum of Fine Arts, Boston, MA
Museum of Modern Art, New York, NY
National Gallery of Art, Washington, DC
Philadelphia Museum of Art, Philadelphia, PA
Smithsonian Institution, Washington, DC
Solomon R. Guggenheim Museum, New York, NY
Walters Art Gallery, Baltimore, MD
Whitney Museum of American Art, New York, NY

SMALLER MUSEUMS

Abby Aldrich Rockefeller Folk Art Center, Williamsburg, VA
Flint Institute of Arts, Flint, MI
Henry Francis du Pont Winterthur Museum, Winterthur, DE
Museum of International Folk Art, Santa Fe, NM

Sterling and Francine Clark Art Institute, Williamstown, MA
Toledo Museum of Art, Toldeo, OH
Worcester Art Museum, Worcester, MA

HOW TO BREAK INTO THE FIELD

College placement services and alumni networks can be of some help. Volunteer work and internships occasionally lead to paying jobs, but these are more often simply opportunities to gain experience and to meet people who can help you farther down the road. The best way is through personal contacts, coupled with demonstrated interest in the field. Because the museum and academic worlds are closely related, ask your professors for suggestions. To say that everyone in the art world knows everyone else is only a slight exaggeration. In museum work, word of mouth and personal recommendations carry great weight, and the more people you know, the better your chances of landing that first job.

The American Association of Museums publishes a monthly newsletter, *Aviso*, which lists job openings. Student membership in the association, which includes a subscription, costs $30, and ensures an invitation to the annual meeting—another excellent place to make contacts. The College Art Association of America publishes a newsletter five times a year that lists job openings. Check your college library or art department for this newsletter.

INTERNATIONAL JOB OPPORTUNITIES

Most foreign museums are operated by national governments, and their policy is to hire their own nationals. In the United States, museum management personnel and those in curatorial positions may travel abroad when arranging loans or supervising traveling exhibitions. Fellowships for museum professionals to study abroad are available, but competition for these is keen.

INTRAPRENEURING

To many people, the words "change" and "museums" seem fairly incongruous. After all, they might reason, museums exist to preserve and commemorate the great works and deeds of the past. On New York's Long Island, there is a museum that has made change an integral part of its collection.

The museum is the Fine Arts Museum of Long Island in suburban Hempstead. A few years back, the museum's executive director, Eleanor Floemhaft, spotted a fledgling trend that she knew would have a major impact in the art world: computer-generated art. After months of thorough investigation into the field, she convinced the museum's board to set aside a section of the institution for displaying computer art from leading artists. She hired as curator of the section Joyce Laskin, an art history major and former school teacher.

Together, Floemhaft and Laskin have established what many consider to be the best representation of computer art in the nation. The museum has added several computers to the display area to allow visitors to try their hands at creating computer art even as they view the exhibits.

The result of the effort: Museum attendance continues to climb, and many of the attendees are school-age children, who as they visit the computer wing also are exposed to the rest of the museum's collection.

ADMINISTRATION

Ideal museum administrators are hard to find. They must have the business acumen to keep their institution efficient and financially sound, but must combine that with a collector's artistic vision and integrity.

Currently, there are not enough people with this double qualification to fill the available posts, and museums have been hiring administrators whose background is in business rather than the arts. If this area of museum work is one that interests you, you would do well to consider working toward a degree in arts administration.

At the entry level, clerical and general office skills are valuable; typing is a must and accounting a plus. Because the administration works with all other departments, an entry-level job gives you a good overview of the way the institution runs and is managed. You'll meet people from every department and become familiar with their work.

At higher levels, administrators budget, oversee bookkeeping, handle requisitions for services and supplies, and process monies to individual departments. Though an administrator's purpose is to build an arts institution rather than to show a profit, this is basically a management job.

QUALIFICATIONS

PERSONAL: Diplomacy. Ability to formulate solutions and delegate responsibility. Ability to conceptualize long-range plans. Financial aptitude.

PROFESSIONAL: Financial and management experience. Accounting and a degree in arts administration particularly helpful.

CAREER PATHS

LEVEL	JOB TITLE	EXPERIENCE NEEDED
Entry	Administrative assistant	College degree
2	Assistant director	5–7 years
3	Director/administrator	7+ years

JOB RESPONSIBILITIES ◆ ENTRY LEVEL

THE BASICS: Typing, filing, answering phones. Processing requisitions for materials. Handling director's correspondence. Bookkeeping. Secretarial duties for other departments when needed.

MORE CHALLENGING DUTIES: Beginning work on budget. Assistance with grant writing and fund raising. Processing and distributing funds throughout museum. Coordinating personnel.

MOVING UP

To win promotion you must demonstrate that you are an exemplary support person: efficient in processing paperwork, accurate with numbers, and able to perform a multitude of clerical tasks with speed and thoroughness. Take accounting and financial management courses: the better you understand budgets and cost efficiency, the more useful you will be to your supervisor. As you move up, you'll begin to have more responsibility for financial planning and for handling personnel.

Because museums have small staffs, advancement is seldom as swift as you'd wish. To move up, it may be necessary to seek a higher-level job at another museum.

CURATORIAL

Curators are responsible for the museum's collection. A curator may work with the entire permanent collection, or may specialize in a certain area—Oriental art, for example—and be responsible only for objects in that category. Curators are responsible for creating catalogs, arranging loans of objects, and, with the administrators, making decisions on building the collection through acquisitions. In the competitive world of museums, curators must keep abreast of new trends in collecting, new areas of research, and new ways to exhibit or store art. They work closely with the conservation staff, which is responsible for preserving and restoring the museum's treasures. Curators also direct the special exhibitions that often attract crowds of art lovers. The curatorial staff may design and arrange an exhibit or, in the case of a large show, they may work with an outside designer. Curators also consult with the education department to create educational programs.

Another function of the curatorial staff, especially entry-level personnel, is research. Detailed records are kept for every artifact and piece of art in the collection. Information gathered for each object includes provenance (the history of its origin and previous ownership), material and medium used, and all pertinent research done on the work and its artist. The curatorial staff does as much research as possible because a collection can only be of full use to scholars and the public if it can be clearly interpreted.

QUALIFICATIONS

PERSONAL: Artistic sensitivity. Intellectual curiosity. Imagination. Ability to write and speak well. Devotion to detail and accuracy.

PROFESSIONAL: Advanced studies in a specialized area of art history. Research experience. Increasingly, the ability to use a word processor. Fluency in reading one, preferably two, foreign languages (French, German, and Italian are preferred).

CAREER PATHS

LEVEL	JOB TITLE	EXPERIENCE NEEDED
Entry	Curatorial assistant/ secretary	College degree
2	Research assistant	3–5 years; advanced study often required
3	Curator	5 years minimum; Ph.D. normally required

JOB RESPONSIBILITIES ◆ ENTRY LEVEL

THE BASICS: Typing curator's reports, correspondence, and manuscripts. Filing accession (acquisition) and curatorial information cards. Writing labels for art objects. Answering phones. Checking facts. General office duties.

MORE CHALLENGING DUTIES: Aiding curator with research, writing up findings, helping fill in curatorial work sheets. Helping hang shows. Writing fact sheets for other departments.

MOVING UP

You will assume responsibility for entire sections of catalogs and begin to investigate areas in the collection that need further research. You will arrange loans, perhaps traveling to work out details. You will also assume responsibility for acquisitions, authorizing the purchase of new objects.

The key to moving up in curatorial positions is to demonstrate excellent research skills and to show initiative in suggesting viable research projects of your own. Find an area of the collection that needs documentation; then, with the approval of your supervisor, do the necessary research. Published research findings, either in museum publications or in art magazines, are invaluable qualifications for being considered for a higher position.

Few top curators have less than an M.A., and many have a Ph.D. Museum curators are a scholarly group, and it's necessary to keep learning all the time. Like academics, they fall victim to the publish-or-perish syndrome. Seminars and conferences are places to make contacts, as well as to keep up with research and current events in the art world. The market for curatorial jobs is often quite tight. To move up, you may need to go from one museum to another.

REGISTRAR

Keeper of all records, repository of all facts about objects in the collection—no museum can function without a registrar. Every object in the collection must have an accession card, telling what it is, when it was acquired, all physical information about the object, and exactly where it is at that moment. Is it on loan? In storage? In the new wing, gallery A, position 7? Is it in the conservation lab? Registrars can tell right away, because they keep all information concerning the objects up to date. The registrar makes arrangements for shipping and loans, and even for moving objects around within the museum. This job may sound simple, but remember that a major museum may have hundreds of thousands of items in storage and on display.

The entry-level position is the assistant. This job requires good clerical and organizational skills. Your knowledge of art history will help you write records and correspondence. This area is increasingly becoming computerized, so the ability to store and retrieve computerized information is a plus.

DEVELOPMENT

Development is one of the fastest growing areas of the museum industry. Rising costs and cutbacks in federal funding have made fund raising more important than ever before.

At one time, curators made their own grant requests, but grant writing has now become a specialty of its own. The development office sponsors individual membership drives, designs corporate membership packages, arranges fund-raising events, such as art shows and benefit balls, and responds to gifts and bequests. Until recently, much of this work had been performed by volunteers, usually museum members. Now museums are hiring people experienced in fund raising for nonprofit organizations. These specialists design the fund-raising programs, which in many cases, are carried out by volunteer museum members.

Fund raising takes energy, belief in your cause, and excellent communication skills. If you enjoy the challenge of financial planning for funds that are far from easy to obtain, development will be an excellent career choice.

EDUCATION

Since museums are assuming greater responsibility now for reaching their public, museum education is a growing area. The education department sponsors classes in studio art and art appreciation, coordinates training programs for tour guides, and arranges tour schedules. In large museums, the education department may produce special shows, films, and slide shows about the collections. In a smaller museum, it will schedule showings of rented films.

The education department also strengthens the institution's ties with the local area by taking traveling lecture series and slide shows out into the community. Some educational programs carry small fees to make some money for the museum, but their primary function is to get people involved with the local art institution.

PUBLICATIONS

A museum publications department is much like a book or magazine publisher. The biggest difference is that the writers and artists will primarily be museum staffers.

In a sense, publications is a service department for the rest of the museum. The publications staff edits, designs, and oversees the publication of scholarly catalogs, annual reports, museum guidebooks, the members' newsletter, brochures about educational programs, and direct mail pieces for the development office. When a museum offers Christmas cards and gift books, these too are developed by the publications department.

Large museums may even have their own presses, but most institutions have small publications staffs. Consequently, you'll have to be proficient in all aspects of publishing, including copyediting and layout, and be able to deal with writers and printers. Often the best way to get into this field is by having publishing experience, especially arts-related, outside of a museum.

PUBLIC RELATIONS

The public relations department is responsible for getting free outside publicity for the museum. This is accomplished in the same way as any other public relations operation—by sending out press releases, staging press events, creating press kits for media representatives who attend them, and dealing with media queries. In addition, the museum's PR department writes and produces public service announcements for radio and television.

In some museums, the public relations function is part of a larger department called public information. This department also produces guidelines and other visitors' information, and handles requests for information about the museum.

SALES

Sales generated by gift shops or mail order catalogs constitute one of the fastest growing sources of income for museums. Once rather amateurishly run, principally by volunteers, these retail outlets are thriving under professionals who employ imaginative marketing techniques.

Large museums produce their own museum-inspired products, such as books, scarves, and jewelry. Smaller museums, which may have no resources to produce replicas and other gifts, can make use of the Museum Store Association to stock their shops. This nonprofit association arranges for items produced in large museums to be retailed by other institutions.

The museum's store may be a department of its own, or it may be run by the development or membership office. Many of the sales staff may be volunteers, but professionals, especially in management positions, are sorely needed. A more complete discussion of this area can be found in the chapter on Art Sales.

CONSERVATION

The conservation department is the domain of the highly trained specialists who preserve and restore works of art. Preservation entails regulating heat and humidity in exhibition and storage areas; ensuring proper lighting to prevent bleaching and fading; overseeing framing, mounting, and hanging; instituting rules for handling objects; and installing and maintaining suitable storage facilities.

Restoration includes repairing and reconstructing ceramics and sculpture, cleaning paintings, repairing torn textiles, cleaning works on paper.

Conservators adhere to a strict code of ethics that ensures the integrity of each object. All repairs must be reversible and visible to the observer. Conservators may reconstruct damaged portions of an art work, but they must remain completely faithful to each artist's intention and refrain from exercising personal style or taste.

Conservation is, above all, a science. The effects of time, pollution, and weather on art is constantly studied and protective measures are devised. A growing variety of chemicals are available to clean and preserve the endless number of media that have been used throughout art history. The conservator is more technician than artist.

The process of becoming a seasoned conservator takes years. Extensive education is required; professionals often have advanced degrees in both chemistry and art, in addition to their training. You begin by performing simple tasks, such as preparing work areas and materials. With close supervision you work first on simple projects, and as your skill and knowledge grow you tackle more complicated tasks.

Many large museums have extensive, sophisticated conservation labs. The staffs in these labs take care of the museum's collection and may also take on outside projects. Many experienced conservators become free lancers, working for smaller museums and private collectors.

ADDITIONAL INFORMATION

SALARIES

Most entry-level jobs pay in the range of $15,500 to $18,500 a year. People with 3–7 years' experience earn from $20,000 to $22,000 a year. Assistant curators start at about $28,000 a year, while curators' salaries are in the mid-thirties to $50,000, and administrators make slightly more. Depending on the museum, some conservators work on a project to project basis, while some have staff positions, so the salaries will vary.

WORKING CONDITIONS

HOURS: Most museum hours are ten to five, five or six days a week, including weekends. If you are in sales, you will certainly work weekends. If you are in the curatorial department, you may work late when hanging shows, and you may have to be in the museum on weekends for openings. No matter what your function, you probably won't leave your work in the office at five o'clock.

ENVIRONMENT: In most museums, the objects have more posh surroundings than the staff. Museum offices are generally cramped, overflowing with files and books. But then again, you may have a fine painting hanging on your wall!

WORKSTYLE: The atmosphere is rather academic, with little of the pressure associated with profit-making businesses. There may be flurries of activity before important shows, at budget time, or before a catalog goes to press, but, in general, work life goes on at a pleasant pace.

TRAVEL: Curators and administrators may travel to other museums around the country, and heads of departments may attend educational workshops. There is virtually no travel at the entry level.

EXTRACURRICULAR ACTIVITIES/WORK EXPERIENCE

Experience as a guide or staff member at any museum, gallery, historic structure, or other cultural institution
Arranging on-campus displays and exhibits
Experience cataloging art works or documents

INTERNSHIPS

Museums are always in need of free labor, so most are happy to sponsor interns. You can gain experience during the summer or part-time during the school year, and sometimes course credit can be arranged. Many large museums have a staff member who hires and places all interns; inquiries should be directed to this person. If you are interested in a particular department and you have some background pertinent to it, consider contacting the department head.

RECOMMENDED READING

BOOKS:

American Art Directory, R.R. Bowker: revised annually

New York's Great Art Museums, by Robert Garrett, Chelsea Green Publishing Co.: 1988

Videodiscs in Museums: A Project and Resource Directory, by Roberta H. Binder *et al.*, Future Systems Inc.: 1987

PERIODICALS

Aviso (monthly), American Association of Museums, 1225 I Street N.W., Ste. 200, Washington, DC 20005

Museum News (bimonthly), American Association of Museums, 1225 I Street N.W., Ste. 200, Washington, DC 20005

PROFESSIONAL ASSOCIATIONS

American Association of Museums
1225 I Street, Ste. 200
Washington, DC 20005

College Art Association of America
275 7th Avenue
New York, NY 10001

American Council for the Arts
1285 Avenue of the Americas
New York, NY 10019

INTERVIEWS

ANNE DUKE
SPECIAL PROJECTS STAFF
METROPOLITAN MUSEUM OF ART
NEW YORK, NY

When I graduated from Colgate University, where I majored in English and art history, I wanted to go into arts administration and work for the National Endowment for the Arts. I took the civil service exam, which is required for any government job, and landed a lucrative position as a proofreader in the Department of Energy. After three weeks, I knew why it paid so well: the work was unbelievably boring! So I went off to take the Radcliffe Publishing Procedures course, where I became interested in book production. Then I moved to New York City and worked in the production department of a small publishing house. After two years there, I worked for a book packager. One year later, I landed my present job at the Metropolitan Museum of Art. At last, I have the job I'd been looking for.

There are seven women in this department, and we are responsible for various printed products sold through the museum store and mail order catalogs. Some of our best-selling items are Christmas cards. We choose the images for the cards and have them printed and distributed. We also do calendars, portfolios, diaries and datebooks. We created a "Metropolitan Cats" calendar, which was a real success. We were so pleased that we were able to capitalize on the fad at its peak.

I never expected working to be so much fun. Can you imagine walking through the Metropolitan every morning to get to your office? I won't get rich here, but other rewards compensate for the salary. I've had a chance to work with people whose intellect and creativity I admire, and to get to know them. I have constant exposure to educational programs at the museum: the seminars, lectures, and visiting scholars. People outside the museum are always interested in what I do. Even if I spend some days poring over printing estimates, museum work does have its glamorous and creative aspects. Most of all, I love what I'm doing. It's been gratifying to find that in the museum world the humanistic interests developed by a liberal arts education are marketable.

GAIL ANDREWS TRECHSEL
ACTING DIRECTOR
BIRMINGHAM MUSEUM OF ART
BIRMINGHAM, AL

I spent the fall of my senior year at the College of William and Mary, getting ready to go to law school. Then one day I saw a notice on a bulletin board for a master's program in history museum studies at Cooperstown Graduate School. I thought it sounded great. I like museums, and I'd majored in history, so I applied and went—with the intention of working at a history museum afterwards. After the one-year program, I received a fellowship to work at Colonial Williamsburg, VA. There, I worked at the Abby Aldrich Rockefeller Folk Art Center. I loved dealing with the objects, and had a wonderful opportunity to work on a book about woven coverlets. I enjoyed Williamsburg, but it's a huge operation, and I was afraid that I wouldn't get much curatorial responsibility for a long time. When the Birmingham Museum of Art invited me to interview for a position as the assistant curator of decorative arts, I went, was offered the job, and accepted.

Birmingham has been a terrific opportunity even though it's a smaller museum and away from the major art centers. As soon as I got here, I realized how little had been done with the permanent collection. The labels were poor, the exhibitions were dull, and there were virtually no publications on the collection. I've been here seven years now, and have published three catalogs on the collection and had three articles published in *Antiques*. You simply don't have the chance to do things like that in a large museum—there is too much bureaucracy and specialization.

I was assistant curator for two and a half years. I was learning constantly about the decorative arts, in the museum and out. I went to the Summer Institute at Winterthur in Delaware, to workshops at the Smithsonian, and to Attingham Summer School in England. A few months after Attingham, I was promoted to assistant director. Soon after, our director left, and I've been acting director ever since. There are only four or five women museum directors here in the States, so this is a tremendous honor for me, especially since I'm only 29. I have decided not to apply for the permanent position. Although I like the conceptual part of this job—the long-term planning, the control—I do miss the curatorial responsibilities. Time I once spent in research is now eaten up by management— meetings with city hall, budgeting, personnel, and the like. But as with every other job in a museum, I'm learning every day. I've started teaching courses at the university, which I really enjoy, and I'm also toying with the idea of writing for an art magazine. I don't know where I'll go from here in terms of my career, but I do know that so far my avocation has been my vocation. I feel very lucky to have a career I've enjoyed so well.

BETSY MCCULLOUGH
MUSEUM SPECIALIST
THE SMITHSONIAN NATIONAL MUSEUM OF AMERICAN
HISTORY
WASHINGTON, DC

I wanted to be a lawyer and I was just about to take the LSATs when I discovered that I just didn't think in a "lawyerly" way. In the mean time I had an internship with a senator to keep up with my political science interests. I had a few months off and I volunteered at the Powell House in Philadelphia. This is a historic house where the first mayor of Philadelphia lived, right next to George Washington at the time of the Revolution. I really enjoyed that experience and I was learning a lot. I also liked the atmosphere.

I worked for the senator during the summer in D.C. and I enjoyed that but I realized that my interests had changed. I decided to go to graduate school in museum studies at George Washington University. I got my master's in museum and academic studies. I learned a lot about American history, which I hadn't studied much of as an undergraduate. During school I worked at a historic house in D.C. part-time giving tours and doing some research. That was a nice balance to graduate school. It wasn't intense—weekends and evenings and maybe two to three short days during the week. I got some work experience. This is important because you need to put in some time and get to know what you want to do. A historic house museum is quite different from a large museum. In a large place you specialize and focus, while in a small place you really have to do everything because there's usually not much staff.

Having done work in two smaller places I had to do an internship for my degree and I decided to try a bigger place so I came to this museum in collections management. This was basically taking care of objects and monitoring their use. I rotated to several different divisions in this museum. This was fun. I spent two or three weeks in each division and I got an overall look at what goes on here. I was hooked on this place after that. As I finished my degree I was offered a part-time job in the education division. I worked with hands-on history objects. This was one of the first and most successful interactive history exhibits. I worked there for nine months. I also had another part-time job at the Supreme Court in the curator's office.

I was going a little crazy with these two jobs, but I was lucky that I was in the Smithsonian. A position opened in the musical history division which was like a dream because I play the flute and I love music. Somehow, I don't know how, I got the job!

I've been here for about a year and a half and it's just been great. I work with the wind instruments and we just received a huge collection of harmonicas which is my current project. I also deal with researchers, instrument makers, and musicians who come here to see our collections. We have a storage space of so many things that are not on exhibit. If people are experts they know what is here and they know what they want to see. I answer letters from people who write to tell us what they have. I also work with donors and put together exhibits. We have a pretty active performance division. I love it because there's so much involved—outside people, inside people, I'm constantly learning.

There are ways to get started. The people who work here have many different stories. I think, if you want to break into the field volunteer experience is invaluable. There are a lot of openings and offerings. In fact the Smithsonian has a new internship policy. When I started you needed a lot of experience to get an internship. Now they are taking younger, less experienced people in order to give them an idea of what the field is like. Get into a museum and don't worry about the pay in the beginning. Most of all, do what you like. I was lucky—things came together for me in a way that was special. There are more and more undergraduate and graduate degree programs in museum studies. The two best, in my opinion, are at Cooperstown and the University of Delaware, but it depends on what you want to emphasize. For example, New York University has a more art-oriented museum studies program. I think the field is becoming more professional, so a graduate degree is not exactly necessary but very important. It depends on the city you are in and your specialization. The art museum and the art history degree is a very different world with its own special requirements and training.

PHOTOGRAPHY

C hances are you've owned a camera since you were a kid, possibly several. You've got albums and boxes filled with snapshots dating from your first bicycle and childhood sweetheart, to shots of your graduation or latest vacation. Photography has been a lot of fun, and in some ways it's been very enlightening, but you need to get back to reality: papers, grades, degree, career.

Not so fast! Photography is a vital part of the working world, and thousands of professionals have used their expertise with cameras to forge lucrative careers as photographers. Think of all the photographs you see every day: in newspapers, books, magazines, advertising brochures, catalogs, and the like. The demand for photographs is such that the cameras never stop clicking.

Of course, it takes more than a camera and a love of taking pictures to make it as a professional photographer. Because photography appeals to so many, the competition for jobs is incredibly intense, particularly in glamour fields like fashion photography and sports photography. News photographers, like their counterparts on the writing side, often start their journalism careers working the overnight shift in smaller towns. That is, if they're fortunate enough to land a full-time job as a staff photographer.

Unless you have a personal connection in the business or have an incredible run of luck, you can expect to spend the first few years of your photography career living a hand-to-mouth type of existence. Jobs may be hard to come by, and the cost of photographic equipment and supplies is high. Many photographers find themselves taking on other work, usually part-time but sometimes full-time, to get through the lean periods.

Photographers themselves fall into two separate categories: staff and free lance. It's difficult to establish a free lance career without a solid background, which usually means experience as a staff photographer, at a corporation, studio, newspaper or magazine, even at a hospital, before striking out on your own.

Photographers depend on a vast support system to maintain and increase their market, and various career options can be found within this support system. There are photo editors, photo researchers, and photo agents. People are needed to staff the stock houses that function as photographic rental libraries. Archival and curatorial work is done in museums and historical societies. Two more options are photo processing and camera repair. Both can be lucrative and rewarding careers, but they require specific and extensive training beyond a B.A. in art.

Technology has created many wonders, and many new jobs, in the world of photography. Stop-action photography and photo microscopy (pictures taken through a microscope) are only two. Advances have also made it possible to transfer visual images over thousands of miles in a matter of seconds, allowing photography to play its part in the growing field of global communications. All this continues to increase the range of careers possible in the photography industry.

JOB OUTLOOK

JOB OPENINGS WILL GROW: Faster than average

COMPETITION FOR JOBS: Keen

NEW JOB OPPORTUNITIES: Medical photography (not to be confused with X-rays) is a new and growing field. One of the largest specialties within it is ophthalmic photography (pictures of the eye). Many major hospitals employ a staff of specialists to provide a visual record of the eye and all its parts. This has been an invaluable tool in helping to track disease and isolate eye functions for study and research. You can write to the Biological Photographic Association in North Carolina for more information regarding all aspects of medical photography. (The address can be found at the end of this chapter.)

The number of magazines devoted to business topics, both general and specific, has risen sharply in recent years. Many business publications hire free lance photographers to take pictures of individuals or business operations. In addition, corporate public relations departments often hire photographers to take photos of executives, new products and the like, which are included in brochures, media press kits, and other packages. Typically, those who take a business-like approach to their work are most favored by these clients.

New job opportunities are also opening up in the area of rights and permissions. In recent years laws have changed in favor of the photographer, who now keeps the rights to his or her shots, no matter how often they're used, unless the photographer chooses to sell those rights. When agents are involved there may be additional stipulations. This, coupled with the vast proliferation of photographs in the media in recent years, has created a complicated legal web. Many large or high volume companies (magazines, stock houses, television networks, etc.) employ people exclusively to keep track of rights and permissions.

GEOGRAPHIC JOB INDEX

For research work, it's imperative to head for the East or West Coast. Some agencies and stock houses are dotted around the country, in places such as Atlanta, GA, Denver, CO, and Albuquerque, NM, but these are small, privately run companies. Because stock houses and agencies exist to service media industries, most of them are in

New York, NY, Los Angeles, CA, and San Francisco, CA. Some can also be found in Chicago, IL.

Work as a photographer can be found anywhere. The choice will depend on what kind of photography you want to do. Newspapers everywhere need photo journalists; brides and grooms everywhere need wedding albums; businesses everywhere need promotional brochures.

For archival and curatorial work the choice will depend on whether your interests are regional or more far-flung. Many small cities and towns have historical societies, but museums with important photography collections are found only in large metropolitan areas.

WHO THE EMPLOYERS ARE

COMMUNICATIONS DEPARTMENTS OF CORPORATIONS employ staff photographers. They supply photos for house organs, intracompany newsletters, promotional brochures, VIP profiles, and annual reports.

THE MEDIA (NEWSPAPERS, MAGAZINES, TELEVISION) are mostly concerned with topical issues. Many of the assignments in this area are given out on a free lance basis, but staff positions can be found.

STOCK HOUSES are photographic rental libraries whose clients are magazines, advertising agencies, book publishers, scholars, and even greeting card companies. Many of the houses specialize in a particular area, such as celebrities, cities and buildings, or topical news items.

PHOTO AGENCIES act as a liaison between free lance photographers and the media. They differ from stock houses in that they represent photographers and often work with them to initiate and carry out specific assignments. They make their profit exclusively through sales.

MUSEUMS AND HISTORICAL SOCIETIES are becoming more and more involved with photographs—for use in exhibits, as historical artifacts, and for reference purposes in their archives.

HOSPITALS employ staff photographers to carry out various specialized medical photography procedures designed to assist physicians. Most large, well-endowed hospitals will hire staff photographers.

PHOTO STUDIOS of various sizes can be found all over the country in urban, suburban, and rural settings. Primarily they do portrait work: weddings, bar mitzvahs, etc.

MAJOR EMPLOYERS

STOCK HOUSES AND AGENCIES
Bettman Archives, New York, NY
Black Star Agency, New York, NY, and Los Angeles, CA
Image Bank, New York, NY
Library of Congress, Washington, DC
Photo Researchers, New York, NY
Time, Inc., New York, NY

MUSEUMS
Center for Creative Photography, Tucson, AZ
George Eastman House, Rochester, NY
International Center of Photography, New York, NY
Museum of Modern Art, New York, NY
Museum of Modern Art, San Francisco, CA

STUDIOS
Bachrach, Boston, MA
J.C. Penney, New York, NY
Sears, Roebuck, Chicago, IL

HOW TO BREAK INTO THE FIELD

A portfolio is the most important thing to have in your possession when you seek work as a photographer. No matter what your background and training, a potential employer will be influenced most by your pictures. It's a good idea to have both a black and white and a color portfolio. Before you assemble it, try to narrow down the area of photography in which you'd most like to work, and use shots appropriate for that field.

To find work as an industrial photographer (this term does not refer to people who take pictures of workers in hard hats building bridges; professionals use the term to describe corporate staff photographers—those photographers who service any particular industry), check with the personnel offices of companies that interest you to see if they employ staff photographers.

You might also get some ideas by looking at trade magazines (listed at the end of this chapter). Many industries and professions depend on photographs to promote their services and products. Reading trade magazines can help you identify potential employers. If any of your teachers have professional connections, now is a good time to make use of them. Chances are there is a photographers' cooperative or association in your city or neighborhood. Phone them, or pay a visit.

For work in stock houses, agencies, or museums, it would be best to contact these organizations directly. Your college employment office can probably be helpful with museums or historical societies, because these jobs are often academically oriented, and some institutions may be associated with colleges and universities.

INTERNATIONAL JOB OPPORTUNITIES

Staff photographers at major magazines and news organizations may have opportunities to travel and work overseas. However, the best chances to remain abroad for long periods of time belong primarily to free lancers.

ENTREPRENEURIAL

Ask someone to name the elements that are essential to a free lance photographer and the first thing they'll mention is a camera. The things that they may not mention, however, could well make the difference between success and failure: a solid portfolio, adequate representation, and sturdy luggage.

Like a graphic artist, a photographer wins clients with his or her portfolio. Obviously, a portfolio should contain a photographer's best work, preferably work that has been sold or published. However, it should also reflect the photographer's full subject range, which could include portraits, landscapes, spot photography, product shots, and the like.

Like good writers or illustrators, good photographers can't sit back and wait for the world to discover them. They need to have their work and talents promoted. Although self-promotion can help land an important job or client, the surest way to get adequate promotion is through an agent. Agencies like Black Star, Gamma Liaison, and Image Bank help many free lance photographers sell their work and find new clients. A number of publishers also offer a venue for "advertising" in portfolio books that are distributed to art directors at book and magazine companies.

As far as the luggage goes, a free lance photographer has to be willing to travel to his or her subject, whether it be by car, train, boat, plane, or camel. The bright side is that clients generally pick up all travel expenses, including hotel bills.

STAFF PHOTOGRAPHY

A photography division is often part of a company's corporate communications, audio-visual, or creative services department. These departments may be responsible for newsletters, client presentations, or promotional literature. There will also be ad hoc assignments, such as photographing the office Christmas party or shooting potential location sites for new branch offices. Assignments will vary according to the kind of company you're working for.

Studio photographers work exclusively with the public. Some of the work is done in-house, and some is done at locations requested by the client, e.g., at ceremonies and receptions. There is not much variation in the work done from day to day. It's virtually all portraiture. However, a consistently high level of quality is necessary to attract and maintain customers. Many studios employ photographer's assistants, so such a position is a good way to get a foot in the door and obtain solid practical training. Although a lifelong career as a studio photographer may not appeal to you because of its limited scope, it can be an excellent bridge to a more rewarding career.

Staff photographers at newspapers and magazines work in a hectic environment, responding daily to news and events. Work on feature-length pieces, or for publications that appear less frequently, is less pressured. But unless you start out with a very small newspaper or magazine, your chances for an entry-level job as a media photographer are almost nil. This is not an area where on-the-job training is provided. You will have to work your way up from small publications or through staff positions in other areas.

A fascinating career is possible as a staff photographer in a hospital, although only well-funded and well-equipped hospitals maintain a photography staff. Photographers are used in the operating room to get shots of surgical procedures, incisions, or body organs. It is a delicate job, requiring both that you learn about specialized equipment and techniques, and that you are able to conduct your work without disturbing doctors as they perform exacting medical procedures.

Staff photographers are expected to know the basics of photo processing and finishing, because many companies have their own darkroom and labs. The size and type of equipment used varies depending on how much of the processing and finishing is done in-house and how much is handled by independent companies. In any case, it will be necessary to have a familiarity with terminology and equipment, even if your skills aren't required.

QUALIFICATIONS

PERSONAL: Intuitive sense of space and design. Manual dexterity. Congenial, good with people. Natural curiosity about the world.

PROFESSIONAL: Detail oriented. Organized and good with follow-through. Ease with photographic equipment and techniques.

CAREER PATHS

LEVEL	JOB TITLE	EXPERIENCE NEEDED
Entry	Trainee	Photography know-how, degree helpful
2	Staff photographer	2–4 years
3	Senior photographer	4–10 years
4	Chief photographer, photo consultant	10+ years

JOB RESPONSIBILITIES ◆ ENTRY LEVEL

THE BASICS: Familiarizing yourself with office, studio, location, or darkroom procedures. Sharpening your skills. Scheduling appointments and maintaining files. Keeping adequate supplies on hand.

MORE CHALLENGING DUTIES: Handling various aspects of projects—either preparing, shooting, or processing. Making your own decisions about lighting and equipment. Suggesting ideas for layout, content, spacing.

MOVING UP

As you improve your skills and demonstrate your reliability and a consistently high quality of work, you'll become responsible for entire projects from conception to completion. You'll begin to oversee other people's work and be responsible for quality control.

When you move from staff photographer to senior photographer you'll design and create assignments, rather than carry them out. You'll be in a position to assign less challenging work to those with less experience and you'll act as a problem solver for other photographers on aesthetic, technical, or tactical considerations.

RESEARCH

Photo research is a relatively new field, conceived primarily to categorize and make accessible the sheer number of photographs that have accrued in the last hundred years. As a researcher you can work in a photo agency, a stock house, or a photo library. Some magazine companies, such as Time, Inc., have such large photo libraries that, besides serving their own needs, they also offer syndication and research services. There is also a fair number of free lance researchers in New York, NY, and Los Angeles, CA, but as with a shooting career, you need substantial experience as a staff person before you can make it on your own. Stock houses abound on the coasts (especially the East Coast), and more and more agencies are springing up to help professional photographers respond to media needs.

A stock house's particular functions will determine its methods of filing. Some files are alphabetized by photographer. Others are categorized by personality files, country files, etc. There are generic files, too ("A" as in animal, "Y" as in youth). As requests for photographs come in, it's up to the researcher to find an appropriate shot. Often the requests do not fall easily into a category. Sometimes people will only hint at what they need, and leave it up to the researcher to hit the nail on the head. There are also specific requests, Frank Sinatra on stage, the Eiffel Tower at night, either you have it or you don't.

Photo agencies have an active relationship with the photographers they represent. The research they do is more along the lines of investigating the market in order to suggest projects for their photographers. Sometimes a photographer will arrive with an idea in mind and the agent will research its feasibility and how the idea might best be implemented. If a photographer wants to do a piece on hunger in America, the agent does the groundwork. The agent finds out where the chief hunger areas are, determines how to get access to subjects, targets and solicits the appropriate media outlet to which to sell the project.

Because nurturing a project takes time and an outlay of expenses, agents need "bread-and-butter" work to sustain them while they develop and negotiate the sale of a project. Selling and reselling popular shots provides this crucial profit cushion.

Another area of research is photo editing, but this is a career path within the publishing industry, and your introduction to it will probably be through another editorial capacity. Photographs often determine newsstand appeal, and the photo editor's job is to establish a visual image for a publication. The job requires a finely tuned aesthetic sensibility, as well as market awareness.

QUALIFICATIONS

PERSONAL: Love of photography. Imagination and resourcefulness. Strong and independent thinker. Articulate.

PROFESSIONAL: Well-organized. An eye for cultural trends. Detail oriented. Aptitude for business and negotiation (for agents).

CAREER PATHS

LEVEL	JOB TITLE	EXPERIENCE NEEDED
STOCK HOUSES AND AGENCIES		
Entry	Researcher	College degree
2	Researcher supervisor	2–3 years
3	General manager	6+ years
AGENCY		
Entry	Agent trainee	College degree
2	Agent	1 year
3	Supervisor/manager	5+ years

JOB RESPONSIBILITIES ♦ ENTRY LEVEL

THE BASICS: In both a stock house and an agency, you'll be required to keep files, answer phones, and handle mail and deliveries.

MORE CHALLENGING DUTIES: In a stock house you'll begin to research requests, initiate searches out-of-house, and develop relationships with particular editors who know they can depend on you for their photo requirements. In an agency you'll be researching project ideas, developing contacts with the media, and scouting new photographers.

MOVING UP

In a stock house as you and your office grow confident in your researching abilities, you'll begin to edit stock and help shape the various files, perhaps suggesting further cross-references. You'll take on responsibility for duplicating prints when necessary, and keeping track of private domain photos and the laws pertaining to their use. You'll also be responsible for scouting new clients to use your company's services, and you'll have a say in handing out assignments.

At an agency, you'll take on more responsibility for particular photographers' work, both recruiting it and selling it. You'll be expected to have a firm grasp on the market and its trends, advising your photographers accordingly. As a supervisor or manager these responsibilities will multiply, and the company will depend on you for quality control.

CURATORIAL AND ARCHIVAL WORK

As photography continues to gain recognition as an art form, major art museums are making an effort to improve their permanent photography collections and to stage exhibitions. The modern art museums in New York, NY, San Francisco, CA, and New Orleans, LA, are especially noted for their excellent photography collections. Many museums around the country are devoted exclusively to photography. Among the most notable are the George Eastman

House in Rochester, NY, and the International Center of Photography in New York, NY. In 1983 the Museum of Photographic Art opened in San Diego, CA.

With photography, the difference between archival work and curatorial work is sharply defined, perhaps more so than with other fine arts. Because of the great numbers of photographs available for use, the curator's task of choosing representative pieces for a show (either of a particular photographer or for a theme exhibit) is monumental. By the same token, an archivist has a prodigious job in categorizing (often with many cross-references), cataloging, and filing thousands of photographs for future reference.

But you don't have to go to a museum to see photographic displays. Many organizations, such as historical societies and chambers of commerce, mount photography exhibits to help generate the interest and support of the community. The number of jobs in this area is increasing all the time. Media centers, such as the Center for Southern Folklore in Memphis, TN, are cropping up all over the country. They unite the arts with various communications outlets and make an effort to keep abreast of trends, mounting holographic (3-D) photography exhibits, for example.

The size of the museum or organization where you get your first job will determine the range of responsibilities you handle. The smaller the place the more likely it is that your initial experience will be broader and more varied. Entry-level assignments in large museums are often more specific and limited in scope.

QUALIFICATIONS

PERSONAL: Aesthetic sensibility. Intrigued with visual images. Cultural and historical curiosity. Unafraid to put ideas into action.

PROFESSIONAL: Well organized. Detail oriented. Work well independently. Knowledge of historical and current trends in photography.

CAREER PATHS

LEVEL	JOB TITLE	EXPERIENCE NEEDED
Entry	Archivist assistant or curatorial assistant	College degree
2	Archivist	3–5 years
3	Archives supervisor	5–10 years
4	Curator	10+ years

JOB RESPONSIBILITIES ♦ ENTRY LEVEL

THE BASICS: Receiving and sorting acquisitions. Arranging for payments on rentals and purchases. Checking facts or information for your superiors.

MORE CHALLENGING DUTIES: Transcribing inscriptions (deciphering photographer's notes written on the back of photos). Documenting and checking inscriptions for authenticity. Helping to mount exhibitions. Framing, hanging exhibitions. Cataloging and filing new acquistions.

MOVING UP

As you acquire a familiarity with the photographs and the work, you'll take on more responsibility for identifying prints when necessary, and cataloging them in terms of their historical context, their subject matter, the type of film, the lighting and equipment used, or technical idiosyncrasies in producing the print. You'll also be responsible for making duplicates of prints. Depending on the facilities at your workplace, you may acquire the skills to do this yourself. But even when this work is done out-of-house, you must know enough to instruct the processors correctly.

The next step is to begin to implement your own ideas for new cross-referencing indexes or possible future exhibits. You'll also begin meeting with dealers and negotiating acquisitions. As a curator, the responsibility for mounting exhibits is entirely yours. This includes writing the exhibit notes and the catalog, procuring and choosing the photographs, and designing the layout and lighting for the exhibit.

ADDITIONAL INFORMATION

SALARIES

An entry-level trainee/staff photographer will make between $16,000 and $25,000 per year. Several years of experience will bring in $24,000 to $29,000 per year. A senior photographer will make $28,000 to $35,000 per year; a chief photographer, $30,000 to $45,000 per year. As a chief photographer you will work for only one company, but a photo consultant works for many companies, and your earnings will reflect the amount of work you take on.

Starting out in an agency or stock house salaries will be from $15,000 to $18,000 per year. In a stock house you will get incremental raises as you take on more responsibility. In agencies your income will rise as you take on your clients and start selling their work, thereby earning commissions.

Salaries are quite low in any kind of curatorial and archival work. Entry-level positions may start at $15,000 to $17,000 per year. Raises may be slow in coming, and dependent on outside sources for funding. But after three years you can expect to make a yearly salary of $18,000 to $25,000, and after five to ten years, between $28,000 and $40,000, depending on your responsibilities.

WORKING CONDITIONS

STAFF PHOTOGRAPHER
HOURS: An office or studio will keep fairly regular business hours, but on those occasions when your assignment caters to a client's time requirements, you may find yourself working early, late, or on weekends.

ENVIRONMENT: You may be in a skyscraper, industrial park, shopping center, or storefront. The offices and studio space will be busy and informal. You'll probably share your work area with at least several other people.

WORKSTYLE: Your time will be divided among location, studio, and darkroom. You'll also spend a fair amount of time in the office, dealing with files and phone requests.

TRAVEL: There will probably be some travel, possibly a lot. Sometimes you'll be gone for a couple of hours, sometimes for a couple of weeks. Your work can take you to Sheboygan or Paris.

RESEARCH

HOURS: In both agencies and stock houses your hours should be fairly regular: nine-to-five, five days a week. If there's pressing business you'll be expected to stay late. As an agent you may find yourself having meetings with photographers or editors over dinner or on weekends.

ENVIRONMENT: The offices will be hectic: phones ringing, colleagues throwing questions at you, clients and photographers coming and going. Stock houses may have some basic computerization of cross references, but most of the work will be done manually so expect a lot of organized clutter. In a stock house or agency, you'll probably start out sharing an office with at least one other person.

WORKSTYLE: You'll spend a lot of time on the phone and with your nose in files. You may spend a portion of your time walking around town making deliveries and pick-ups. Libraries, museums, galleries, historical societies, and other photographic resources will become well-known terrain. This will help you sound out your knowledge in particular areas and give you ideas for acquisitions for your own files.

TRAVEL: There is almost no call for travel as a researcher or agent. All your long-distance work can be done by phone or mail.

CURATORIAL AND ARCHIVAL WORK
HOURS: You'll keep fairly regular nine-to-five hours on work days, unless an opening is coming up. Then you may find yourself working as much as 20 extra hours a week to help with its preparation.

ENRIVONMENT: Depending on the size and type of organization you work for, you may be in a back office at a huge museum, at a media center in a shopping mall, or on a village street corner, or perhaps in a Victorian mansion that houses the town historical society. These places will be open to the public, but you'll work behind the scenes, usually in shared office space.

WORKSTYLE: In the beginning you'll spend a lot of time at the files, familiarizing yourself with stock and procedures. You'll also be on the phone taking queries, and tracking down information.

TRAVEL: There won't be a call for travel in your first couple of years. But as you gain responsibility you may go to other cities to see exhibits or meet with out-of-town dealers.

EXTRACURRICULAR ACTIVITIES/WORK EXPERIENCE

Staff photographer for yearbook, campus newspaper, or campus magazine
Audio-visual assistant; projectionist
Summer or part-time job in local camera shop, processing lab, or photo studio

INTERNSHIPS

Many museums offer internships, including the ones listed here under "Major Employers." Contact museums directly or check the many internship catalogs available at the library or your school's placement office.

Free lance photographers often hire unpaid apprentices. This can be an arduous job—lugging equipment, keeping track of film and contact sheets, setting up appointments. But with this hands-on experience you can learn how professional photographers work technically, what results they get from different kinds of equipment, how they achieve quality in their work, and how they conduct themselves professionally. You can also tap resources that can help you move into a salaried position later on.

RECOMMENDED READING

BOOKS

The Foreign Syndication Handbook, by Vickie M. Comiskey, Haberman Press: 1987

Photographer's Market, Robert Lutz, ed., Writers Digest Books: revised annually

Promoting Yourself as a Photographer, by Frederic W. Rosen, Watson, Gupthill: 1987

Starting and Succeeding in Your Own Photography Business, by Jeanne C. Thwaites, Writers Digest Books: 1984

PERIODICALS

Industrial Photographer (monthly), United Business Publications, 475 Park Avenue South, New York, NY 10016

News Photographer (monthly), National Press Photographers Association, 3200 Croasdale Drive, #306, Durham, NC 27705

Photo District News (monthly), Visions Unlimited, 49 East 21st Street, New York, NY 10010

Photodesign (bimonthly), Billboard Publications, 1515 Broadway, New York, NY 10036

Photomethods (monthly), Professional Photographers of America, 1090 Executive Way, Des Plaines, IL 60018

The Professional Photographer (monthly), 1090 Executive Way, Des Plaines, IL 60018

PROFESSIONAL ASSOCIATIONS

American Society of Magazine Photographers (ASMP)
419 Park Avenue South
New York, NY 10016

INTERVIEWS

SCIENTIFIC AND TECHNICAL PHOTOGRAPHER
U.S. NAVY
VIRGINIA BEACH, VA

I went to Old Dominion University in Norfolk, where I got a B.S. in industrial education, with an emphasis in graphics. I also have a master's in supervision and management.

I taught graphics and photography in high school, and within a few years I was teaching photography exclusively. I designed the photography curriculum for the entire Norfolk school system. From there I became media coordinator for the junior high school system, which involved PR photography, photo stories, slide series, and so on. I was responsible for most presentations that required photographic work.

I am still involved in teaching—I teach photography at Tidewater Community College and serve as an adviser in the development of the photography curriculum—but my main job is working with the Navsea Audio Visual Production Center. I was recently hired to direct the Media Program Center, and my official title is scientific and technical photographer. I photograph ships—from the smallest component to the whole. This work is in support of the educational program. My photographs illustrate the training manuals for the shipyard apprenticeship modernization program.

A lot of my time is spent in planning for our photography needs. These are books that are used at shipyards all over the country, so we have to be confident about what we're doing. I work very closely with the writers of these manuals, figuring out exactly what points need illustrating and what type of photos are required. I do most of the actual shooting myself. Because I know what's needed for an illustration, it's best for me to go out and get it personally. So much is lost in trying to communicate verbally the subtleties required in a particular photograph—a problem I avoid by doing the work myself.

For instance, we recently did a whole series on boiler repair, and a great deal of time was spent in the planning stages. I can find myself, literally, in some pretty tight places, wearing coveralls, a hard hat, and other safety gear, as I get at the inner workings of the ship. If we need very detailed, well-lit photos of, say, a valve or a pump, we usually dismantle the object and shoot it in the laboratory.

The training program also uses video presentations. It's my responsibility to choose stills from the video to illustrate the manuals that accompany these presentations.

My favorite aspect of this job is seeing the finished project. Every aspect of each job, concept, design, writing, illustration, production, is done by me or the people I work with. It's exhilarating to have the fruits of our labor in hand.

STAN ROWAN
PRINCIPAL OWNER AND PHOTOGRAPHER
STANLEY STUDIO
BOSTON, MA

I had a camera and I was taking pictures as a child and all through high school. I went to college, studied engineering, and then I received an M.B.A. at Boston University. I became a sales manager for a large sales company in Cambridge. I realized that I had always wanted to be artistic in some way. I couldn't play the piano and I couldn't draw, but I always had a camera. I felt I could do it, so I quit the executive world and decided to become a photographer. I assisted photographers and I interned for a couple of years and then I went out on my own. Now I do mostly advertising and commercials, editorial pictures, and photographs for magazines.

If you want to get started in photography you have to first decide what type of photographer you want to be. You have to set that goal in your mind—what kind of pictures do you want to take? You can take fashion pictures, you can do art, you can take people and still-lifes. Then you have to, somehow or another, be different than the other four or five thousand, actually probably more like ten thousand, professional photographers. You have to be different than everyone else in order to create a niche for yourself. You have to exploit your little creativity.

I have been successful as a photographer for a number of reasons. I was in the right place at the right time. I get along with people. It was a slow process. There are superstars who do it right away. They have their own distinct eye and people see that, recognize it, and these photographers are out in front immediately. These guys are usually in their twenties. Then there are the ones like me who are just doing it slowly and steadily, going from door to door, showing their stuff. My clients are ad agencies and design firms. I have to go from firm to firm, showing my work. They don't come to you, so it's not quick and easy for me—it's slow and hard.

There are parts of the business that are more lucrative than other parts. Magazine photography pays the least. In fact anything that's glamorous pays the least. Fashion photography and magazine portraits pay almost nothing. The cover of the *New York Times Magazine* will pay between $500 and $800, and that might take you three days to shoot. On the other hand, if you shoot something for an ad and you get no credit for it, they will pay you three or four thousand dollars for the same amount of time. Advertising pays a lot more, but you get little exposure and no public gratification. Wedding photography and portrait photography pays somewhere in the middle and it takes more technical training. But I don't know of many people who want to just do that kind of photography.

If I were getting started today, and I did not have a degree in photography, I would pick up a camera, I would learn how to use it, and then I would go out and take pictures. Then I would look to see what kind of pictures I enjoyed taking and I would specialize in that area—concentrating on just those pictures. I'd then build up a small portfolio of those pictures I was happy with and I'd go around and show them to people who hire that type of work—be it newspapers or art galleries or magazines.

In order to be a photographer you have to have a tiny ego and be able to take lots of abuse. Or you have to have a big ego and give a lot of abuse. There are all sorts of personalities in photography. Obviously, you have to be creative and there's a niche for every kind of personality, so who you are is not that important. You just have to be patient.

My advice to a young person who wants to be a photographer is to find a different career. Teach English. Right now in Boston, there is a tremendous pulling back in advertising from creative work. One business after another is going out of business. If you really enjoy this then just keep on doing it, and don't pay attention to what anyone says. If you have to wait on tables, fine, but keep on taking pictures. You don't have to have an M.F.A. to be a photographer, unless you want to teach. The best way to learn is to assist other photographers. I've got $40,000 worth of equipment and nobody starting out can afford that. There aren't books written about how to work the equipment, so you have to just learn from a professional. I'm constantly hiring free lance assistants, some of whom have no experience. I just like them. I teach them how to work the cameras and they move out and do it on their own. There are trade schools, but why pay to learn when someone can pay you to learn. It's really an apprenticeship system.

ART SALES

The wisdom of the ages—or at least the 20th century—holds that the most intelligent place to invest one's money is in real estate. Of course, that wisdom is relative. An acre of central Florida swampland isn't likely to be much more valuable 20 years from now than it is today. However, a sketch by Picasso or an oil painting by Degas—well, that's another story.

As distressing as it may be to connoisseurs, fine art has taken its place beside lots and acreage, stocks and bonds, and other such components of the investment portfolio. Big names bring the biggest bucks. Several masterworks have already commanded more than $15 million, and the trend shows no sign of abating. Put up a van Gogh for auction at Sotheby's, and you're sure to attract a host of buyers, many of them corporations, and many of them from Japan, who seem hell-bent on outbidding one another for the prize.

Although the art business continues to command headline attention with megadeals, the heart of the business continues to be the small gallery and auction house. Corporations are buying art, but corporate America itself has so far kept out of the business of selling art. Although a number of galleries and auction houses are considered to be major, they are, of course, minuscule compared to the multinational conglomerates.

Galleries are springing up in every major city in the country.

Although New York, NY, is still generally recognized as the center for both the American and international art markets, other areas in the United States are becoming important both as sources and resources for art and as places where art ideas can be exchanged. These include Los Angeles, CA, San Francisco, CA, Washington, DC, Chicago, IL, Boston, MA, Philadelphia, PA, and the Dallas–Fort Worth, TX area, as well as a host of smaller cities.

The use of computers is more the rule and less the exception in even modest-size galleries. For years, museums, auction houses and galleries with international branches have been adapting computer technology to their needs. At the present time other art establishments are either already computerized or are making plans to be. Your chances of getting a job in any art establishment are enhanced if you can already use a computer or are prepared to learn how to use one.

The computer is used for payroll, billing, inventory control, keeping tabs on the arrival of lots in an auction house, maintaining mailing lists, coordinating activities at various branches, and keeping track of items that are on the market through other establishments. The use of the computer is rarely limited to what the establishment originally expected, so personnel who operate these computers are also expected to be able to learn new applications as needs arise.

JOB OUTLOOK

JOB OPENINGS WILL GROW: Faster than average.

COMPETITION FOR JOBS: Keen

NEW JOB OPPORTUNITIES: It remains to be seen whether the boom in art sales is recession-proof. As long as the economy remains reasonably healthy, however, art sales should continue to grow, although it may be too much to expect the astronomical jumps achieved in the 1980s. As long as the boom continues, however, galleries, auction houses, and other sellers of art (both originals and reproductions) will continue to need qualified art experts. Many employers are looking for people with specialized knowledge of a certain genre, medium, or period. In-depth knowledge of a specific area could be your foot in the door to a rewarding opportunity.

GEOGRAPHIC JOB INDEX

The bulk of the jobs in art sales will be found in New York, NY, and other major cities in the United States. However, there are important galleries and museums in many places, including Taos, NM, Palm Beach, FL, Boulder, CO, Ann Arbor, MI, and Laguna Beach, CA. Department stores and mail order houses are located in major cities.

WHO THE EMPLOYERS ARE

ART GALLERIES show and sell the works of artists. Generally a gallery will specialize in a certain medium—paintings, sculpture, objets d'art—or a period, school, or style of art.

AUCTION HOUSES sell works of art for owners at auction or sometimes directly.

MUSEUMS sell copies of objects either on loan or on permanent display in their collections. Museum shops are usually located on the premises of the museum, although some may have additional outlets in their city.

DEPARTMENT STORES sell good original art as well as fine reproductions in art departments that employ highly qualified persons as buyers and require knowledgeable sales personnel to deal with an increasingly sophisticated clientele.

MAIL ORDER HOUSES sell works of art through catalog sales. They are almost always attached to a gallery, auction house, department store, or art consultant firm.

MAJOR EMPLOYERS

ART GALLERIES
Biltmore Gallery, Los Angeles, CA
Blumka, New York, NY
Delahunty, Dallas, TX
Wally Findlay, New York, NY
Hirschberg, Boston, MA
Hirschl & Adler, New York, NY
Mission Gallery, Taos, NM
Van Doren, San Francisco, CA
Wildenstein, New York, NY
Worthington, Chicago, IL

AUCTION HOUSES
Christie's, New York, NY
William Doyle, New York, NY
Phillips, New York, NY
Sotheby Parke Bernet, New York, NY
(Branches of these houses can be found in major cities in the United
    States and abroad.)

MUSEUMS
Art Institute of Chicago, Chicago, IL
The Guggenheim Museum, New York, NY
Metropolitan Museum of Art, New York, NY
Museum of Fine Arts, Boston, MA
Museum of Modern Art, New York, NY
Museum of Natural History, New York, NY
Philadelphia Museum of Art, Philadelphia, PA
San Francisco Museum of Modern Art, San Francisco, CA
The Smithsonian Institution, Washington, DC
Whitney Museum of American Art, New York, NY

DEPARTMENT STORES
B. Altman, New York, NY

Federated Department Stores and Allied Stores Corporation,
Cincinnati, OH (parent company for Jordan Marsh, Blooming-
dale's, Abraham & Straus and others)
R. H. Macy & Company, New York, NY
Neiman, Marcus, Dallas, TX
Sears, Roebuck & Company, Chicago, IL

HOW TO BREAK INTO THE FIELD

Your first job in the art world may not necessarily be one in sales. It
could be volunteering at a museum shop, being a go-fer for a small
gallery owner, or working in your university gallery in your spare
time. Contacts are the most important thing you can cultivate when
looking for a job in art sales. Make a point of attending shows,
meeting artists, dealers, brokers, gallery owners. Although some
jobs may be advertised in the classified sections of the newspaper
(under galleries, auctions, art dealers), the majority of jobs, especially in galleries, are known only through word of mouth. Any
sales experience, even in a field not remotely related to art, is a plus.
Before writing to gallery owners, the personnel departments of
museums or auction houses, or the heads of the department store
art departments, familiarize yourself with their operations. Include
in your letter of introduction the reasons why you would be
especially useful to their organization. Enclose a résumé and follow
up on your letter with a phone call.

INTERNATIONAL JOB OPPORTUNITIES

Overseas travel is unlikely in an entry-level position, but as you
move up, the responsibilities for foreign travel increase. Galleries
look abroad for the works of new and established artists; auction
houses sometimes require the services of an expert to authenticate
pieces being offered abroad. Department store buyers occasionally
travel abroad to inspect collections.

GALLERIES

Galleries display and sell works of art. A show of a particular artist's
work or work of a certain style or with a unifying theme is mounted

by the gallery. The public is invited by personal invitation (usually for the opening, which can be an important social event) or through newspaper and magazine advertising. A show may hang for weeks or months, depending on the size of the gallery, the reputation of the artist or artists involved, and the significance of the show in terms of art history or current art trends.

Even the largest, most influential galleries with several branches are intimate places. The tone of the establishment is set by the personal preferences and tastes of the owner. The clientele of a gallery will generally share those tastes and preferences. Your understanding of this will greatly affect your progress in the art world. If you respond most strongly to abstract art, you probably will not do well in a gallery that specializes in Impressionists. If you are interested in selling works done in the style of the moment you will not succeed in an establishment where the clientele wants a painting that first of all must match the living room decor.

ART SALES/ENTREPRENEURIAL

It takes a lot to start an art gallery—a lot of money, a lot of time, a lot of patience, a lot of experience. Given all that, however, gallery ownership is probably the best entrepreneurial path in the business of selling art.

The best way to start on this path is to get a few years' worth of experience at an established gallery. Get to know the inner workings of the gallery; how shows are set up, how finances are arranged, how bills are paid, and so on. Keep your eye out for emerging trends among buyers and undiscovered talent that shows promise. Get to know buyers and artists, and more importantly, make sure they get to know you.

Probably the most critical factor that determines the success or failure of a gallery venture is location. A gallery is sure to get more knowledgeable browsers and potential customers in an area like the SoHo section of Manhattan, but the competition there is stiff and the rents have become astronomical.

Rather than try to make it as small fish in a big pond, a number of gallery owners have set up successful enterprises in areas that are seemingly far from the art world's mainstream. Resort areas are home to many thriving galleries. Vacationers tend to have the money to buy art, and vacations tend to put people in a spending mood. Such galleries often specialize in showing works from regional artists.

QUALIFICATIONS

PERSONAL: A love of art. A personable disposition. A good memory for names and faces. The ability to remain calm and composed under pressure.

PROFESSIONAL: Knowledge of art, artists, techniques, and materials. The ability to speak to clients about art without seeming superior or overly technical. The ability to deal with many sorts of people.

CAREER PATHS

LEVEL	JOB TITLE	EXPERIENCE NEEDED
Entry	Sales assistant	College degree, sales experience helpful
2	Assistant manager	1–3 years
3	Manager	4–6 years
4	Owner or partner	7–10 years, plus financial backing and excellent contacts in the art world

JOB RESPONSIBILITIES ♦ ENTRY LEVEL

THE BASICS: Typing, filing, telephone work. Sending out invitations to shows. Maintaining and updating mailing lists. Keeping track of inventory.

MORE CHALLENGING DUTIES: Direct contact with customers and artists.

MOVING UP

Many moves will be made laterally, that is, you might become a sales assistant at a larger, more prestigious gallery after a stint at a modest gallery. It cannot be emphasized too strongly that contacts will enable you to move to more responsible positions. To be promoted to assistant manager and then to manager, you will need to demonstrate administrative abilities in staff management and the business end of the work.

The step to a partnership or owning a gallery can only be taken after you have established a solid and widely known reputation in the field. You may be able to start a small gallery with comparatively little money if the gallery fills a need that has not yet been met, for example, serving an area that could support a gallery but does not have one, showing the work of up-and-coming artists, showing works of a brand-new style or trend.

AUCTION HOUSES

Many of the world's most important pieces of art, jewelry, furniture, and other objects move through auction houses when they pass from one owner to another. In some cases, entire estates are consigned for sale through an auction house, in others, a single rare miniature or African mask may be offered.

Before each auction sale, invitations are sent to the establishment's regular clientele, which includes dealers and brokers as well as private collectors. Catalogs may be sent along with the invitations, but more often these are purchased by potential bidders when they arrive to examine the lots that are being offered. (A lot is an object or group of objects.) As bidders enter the auction room they are assigned a number and given a card corresponding to that number. During the actual bidding, they hold up that card to indicate their willingness to meet the opening price or an increment. Before the auction the seller and the house often agree on a starting bid. The lot will not be sold for less than that amount. Occasionally there will be voice bidding, but most houses prefer the card system because it allows the auctioneer easily to identify clients with whom he or she is not personally acquainted.

The functions within an auction house are diverse: objects must be examined, appraised, and authenticated; copy must be researched and prepared for catalogs; mailing lists must be maintained; auctions must be planned and advertised; inventory and accounts must be managed. Auction houses also do some direct selling on a consignment or commission basis, and most of them carry on a large mail order business. Life is apt to be hectic before and during a major sale, and even without a large operation in the works there is likely to be a certain amount of well-organized chaos. The work is hard and demanding, but exciting and rewarding as well.

QUALIFICATIONS

PERSONAL: Energy and stamina. Ability to work well under pressure. An eye for detail. A pleasing personality. Natural curiosity and continual desire to increase your knowledge. Extremely good organization.

PROFESSIONAL: Thorough grounding in art history. Cataloging and computer skills.

CAREER PATHS

LEVEL	JOB TITLE	EXPERIENCE NEEDED
Entry	Assistant	College degree
2	Assistant manager	2–3 years
3	Manager	5–10 years

JOB RESPONSIBILITIES ♦ ENTRY LEVEL

THE BASICS: Typing, filing, taking telephone queries. Cataloging lots for less important auctions.

MORE CHALLENGING DUTIES: Direct contact with customers. Beginning to specialize in a certain area, or preliminary training as an auctioneer.

MOVING UP

One way of garnering a more responsible position is to become a specialist, particularly in an area that is both up-and-coming and short of people with in-depth knowledge. Keeping your eye out for such specialty areas and educating yourself in them can help you move up quickly. Showing a talent for administration of staff and business details can also get your career moving. If auctioneering is your goal, look for any opportunity to officiate at even the smallest sale. In many states, auctioneers must be licensed. If you demonstrate good potential as an auctioneer—an excellent memory, the ability to oversee rapid simultaneous events—your employer will see that you are trained in the skills necessary to pass the auctioneer examination.

MUSEUMS

At one time museum shops were pokey little affairs staffed by volunteers, offering picture postcards and souvenir publications. Today the picture has changed, as have the pictures in the shop. A museum shop is as likely to be staffed with paid professional sales personnel as any other art store, and its operations are as likely to be guided by sophisticated marketing and research techniques as any other successful commercial enterprise.

Museum shops sell books, catalogs, quality reproductions of paintings and objects on exhibit, calendars, appointment books, jewelry, posters, and the ubiquitous postcards. Many shops have mail order outlets. In this time of rising costs and decreased funding, museum shops are providing an important source of revenue for their institutions. Knowledgeable personnel are needed to staff and manage the shops, to buy merchandise, or to create merchandising ideas.

QUALIFICATIONS

PERSONAL: Warm, outgoing nature. Patience. Love of art and museums. Well-organized.

PROFESSIONAL: Good knowledge of art and artists, and especially of the museum's collections. Knowledge of sales and retailing techniques. Ability to set up attractive displays. Clerical and computer skills helpful.

CAREER PATHS

LEVEL	JOB TITLE	EXPERIENCE NEEDED
Entry	Sales assistant	College degree, sales experience helpful
2	Assistant manager	1–3 years
3	Manager	5–7 years

JOB RESPONSIBILITIES ♦ ENTRY LEVEL

THE BASICS: Keeping stock in order and in good supply. Clerical duties, such as typing, filing, and answering the phone. Keeping records of orders and sales.

MORE CHALLENGING DUTIES: Ordering stock. Working with artists or artisans who create the reproductions. Offering ideas for new items.

MOVING UP

A museum shop will be successful if it is able to supply the museum-going public with satisfying merchandise. This means constantly upgrading your knowledge of the museum's permanent collections and special shows. You can move up by perceiving gaps in the shop's stock and proposing new items, by coming up with good ideas for merchandise tied in with special shows, or by offering solutions to current merchandising problems. Demonstrating administrative abilities will also enhance your chances of moving into a managerial position.

DEPARTMENT STORES

Several years ago the mail order division of Sears Roebuck & Company hired Vincent Price, the actor and art collector, to act as their art consultant and spokesperson. Price advised the company on buying quality art, including fine reproductions, which it then offered through its well-known catalog. This became one of the most successful experiments in the mass marketing of artworks.

For years department stores have sold prints, paintings, and quality reproductions. Some stores have also sold rare or unique books, antique maps, limited edition lithographs, antique furniture, or other specialty items. Most of these departments do an excellent mail order trade in addition to sales at the store.

Often sales personnel will be hired on the basis of their ability to sell well; an art background is considered of secondary importance. However, in order to work your way up to being a buyer, a thorough knowledge of art and antiques is required.

There are also specialty shops that offer well-crafted jewelry, home decoration accessories, paintings, reproductions, and prints. In addition to these there are shops that sell only one specialized item or group of items—miniatures, Russian enamels and Fabergé eggs, hand-painted wallpaper, and so forth. These shops, like the department stores, do a great deal of mail order business, selling through catalogs or other direct mail publications.

As in all aspects of art sales, computers are becoming increasingly important in keeping track of the objects being offered for sale. Art objects are often secured through dealers or other individuals, rather than through wholesalers or manufacturers. Therefore there is a great deal of record-keeping that the computer facilitates. Some department stores and specialty shops are using computers to keep abreast of trends, because successful selling in these areas entails knowing what to sell as much as how to sell it.

ART CONSULTANT

An art consultant advises a potential buyer on art purchases. More often than not the buyer is not an individual but represents a corporation, an industrial complex, a hotel, or other institution. While this is in no way an entry-level position, there are jobs available as assistants to art consultants. It is also an area that is expected to grow and may be a place on which to set your sights for the future.

The consultant works with the client, considering the many elements that will affect purchasing: the budget, the decor and architectural design of the building into which the works of art will be placed; the people who will be surrounded by the works; the image the client wishes to present. Often the client will want the artworks to reflect regional characteristics.

Besides having a thorough knowledge of art, the consultant should be well-versed in the principles of interior design, should know dealers and artists, and should be aware of developments in corporate and industrial settings. The job requires you to be as much psychologist as salesperson. It is an expanding field and could offer graduates with the right blend of art savvy and business ability a promising new career choice.

ADDITIONAL INFORMATION

Entry-level salaries at galleries are low, ranging from $15,000 to $18,000 per year. However, there is often an opportunity to increase your earnings through commissions, especially as your selling skills improve. Assistant managers earn between $18,000 and $22,000; managers can make $28,000 and up, depending on the size, prestige, and location of the gallery. Owners can make well into six figures.

At auction houses entry-level people also earn $15,000 to $18,000 a year; assistant managers (also known as technical assistants) up to $23,000; managers (or department heads) upward of $30,000. In some cases auctioneers are paid on commission; in others they are salaried. They earn as much as, and often more than managers.

Museums are not known for their high salaries. Entry-level personnel are often paid by the hour and can expect between $6 and $7 per hour. Assistant buyers can make $20,000 to $22,000 a year, buyers $28,000 and up, while top managerial personnel make $40,000 to $50,000 per year.

WORKING CONDITIONS

HOURS: Expect some evening and weekend hours in all entry-level art sales positions. Strict nine-to-five hours are as rare as a newly discovered van Gogh.

ENVIRONMENT: Every gallery will be different—some stark and modern, others appointed with fine antiques. Behind-the-scenes arrangements, where you will do a lot of your work, can also vary, but in general you will have a desk although not an office of your own. In auction houses, entry-level people will share working space, although you will have your own desk, telephone, and sometimes computer terminal. In museum stores, department stores, and other stores, you will be on the selling floor and will have a desk in the office area.

WORKSTYLE: In galleries you will shuttle back and forth between the display area and the office. The desk in the selling area is for convenience when writing up sales. During most of your selling time you will want to be circulating among the customers. At auction houses most of your time will be spent at your desk, meeting with colleagues, or in the display areas. There will also be days when you dress in your oldest jeans and poke around a storeroom examining a new lot of merchandise. In stores you will be on the selling floor with customers, or at your desk taking care of paperwork. As a buyer you will be meeting with dealers, artists, and other suppliers, generally at their place of business.

TRAVEL: There will be little travel for entry-level employees, but as you move up the opportunities increase. Gallery employees sometimes travel to other cities or countries to attend shows, meet artists, or buy works. Auction houses often have branches abroad (in fact, some are based abroad) or in other cities to which you will travel to authenticate a piece, assist with a major auction, or learn new companywide procedures. Museum and store employees will have the chance to travel to acquire new items for sale in their shops.

EXTRACURRICULAR ACTIVITIES/WORK EXPERIENCE

Volunteer work in museums—as a guide, in membership drives, in
   community outreach programs
Student assistant in university art gallery
Sales experience in any area

RECOMMENDED READING

BOOKS
Art Sales Index, Richard Hislop, ed., Apollo Books: revised annually

Career Opportunities in Art, by Susan H. Hauberstock and David Joselit, Facts on File Inc.: 1988

This Business of Art, by Diane Cochrane, Watson Gupthill Publications Inc.: 1988

PERIODICALS
American Artist (monthly), Billboard Publications, 1515 Broadway, New York, NY 10036

Antiques Magazine (monthly), Brant Publishing, 980 Madison Avenue, New York, NY 10021

Art in America (monthly), 980 Madison Avenue, New York, NY 10021

ARTnews (monthly), 48 West 38th Street, New York, NY 10018

Artweek (weekly), 1628 Telegraph Avenue, Okaland, CA 94612

PROFESSIONAL ASSOCIATIONS

American Associations of Museums
1225 I Street, N.W., Ste. 200
Washington, DC 20005

American Crafts Council
40 West 53rd Street
New York, NY 10019

American Society of Appraisers
535 Herndon Parkway
Herndon, VA 22070

Art and Antiques Dealers League of America
353 East 78th Street, Ste. 19A
New York, NY 10021

Art Dealers Association of America
575 Madison Avenue
New York, NY 10022

INTERVIEWS

ASSISTANT, DEPARTMENT OF IMPRESSIONIST AND MODERN PAINTING
AUCTION HOUSE
NEW YORK, NY

I was graduated from college with a B.A. in art history and French. I have found the fact that I can speak and write French enormously helpful in my work. We do a great deal of corresponding in French and I often have to use the language both in dealing with clients and in doing the research that's needed before an estimate is made. I don't speak German, which is another good language to know in this field, but I'm able to read it, which helps.

My entry-level job here three years ago was in the marketing division. Although I have been in the modern painting department only about a year, it wasn't an entry-level move from one department to another in the strictest sense because I already knew many of the clients and was aware of the procedures. What has happened since coming into the painting department is that I'm learning more, both in a procedural sense and about art.

The sales process is usually initiated by a letter or phone call from an owner who tells us about the piece. He or she may send in a photograph. If the owner decides to go ahead with the sale based on what we say at that time—for example, if the piece is by a well-known artist and seems to be in good condition, a possible price may be mentioned—I meet with the seller and we bring the painting in.

We then research the literature on the work. I may assist the cataloger in researching the painting and the artist. If not enough information about either is available, I contact the experts for advice. When all the information is in, we can then make an estimated sales price which the seller can either accept, and decide to go ahead with the sale, or reject.

The job keeps me busy but I still get around to art shows and museums. For one thing, I enjoy doing this; I always have. For another, it's part of my job to be aware of what is being shown, and also to learn more about the lesser-known artists who you don't usually come across in conventional art history courses. I'm also learning to appreciate these lesser-known works, which adds to my personal satisfaction as well as to my professional knowledge.

GENIE SIMMONS
ADMINISTRATIVE ASSISTANT
GROGAN AND COMPANY, INC.
BOSTON, MA

I majored in English in college and I got started by working part-time at an auction house here at Grogan and Company. Generally, the way most people get started in this field is by starting at the bottom. It's common to start part-time at an auction house and you slowly become more familiar with the systems. When a position opened up full-time I applied for that.

There's a lot of paper work that goes on behind the scenes at auction houses. So there's paper work when people bring in items to be consigned, when there is a buyer, and after the item has been sold. I assist with setting up the files for purchases and consignments and I deal with the clients when they come in. In the auction house business, we're officially called auctioneers *and* fine art appraisers. So there is the appraisal side. We do appraisals for insurance purposes, for estates, for law firms, for banks, and for private individuals. You might be going into a home to look at items that are going to be sold at auction, getting auction estimates, or you might be appraising for donation purposes.

The best way to move up in the field is to first learn market values. That is knowledge you can only get by being in the field, you can't learn it at school. There are two ways: you could get a Ph.D. in the field and take an academic approach to your specialty, be it paintings or furniture, or a more common way, is to jump into the field and learn on the job. You can learn how to appraise things by being around experts who already have the knowledge and paying attention to current market values (prices at auction). Because, when people are consigning things you are basically giving them information about what the item is, and what you expect the price will be at auction. The history and origin are of interest, but most importantly it is the prospective price.

I like being around the objects, being around the antiques and thinking about the history that surrounds them—why the people used the objects that they did. I'm also interested in the place and time. It is just fascinating to think about the past. A person who goes into this field should be fascinated with history and objects and be a collector. The job is also a very people-oriented business, because you learn a lot from people who are already in the field. They may be private collectors or dealers as they buy a lot at auctions. It is a constant exchange of information. There's always the hope you are going to discover that undiscovered treasure that is very valuable and might make someone wealthy. That dream keeps a lot of people in the business. The fun part is you never know when you're going into someone's house what you may find.

I would advise someone who wants to get into the business to apply for internships and entry-level jobs in the field. You call the appropriate auction house and figure out who is in charge of hiring interns. There is usually a specific person. Most people work their way up. It's not uncommon to start at the bottom and there are jobs available because there is a certain amount of turnover in the business.

BIBLIOGRAPHY

The American Almanac of Jobs and Salaries, by John W. Wright, Avon Publishers: 1989

American Art Directory, R. R. Bowker: revised annually

Art Career Guide, by Donald Holden, Watson-Guptill Publications: 1983 •

Career Opportunities in Art, by Susan H. Hauberstock and David Joselit, Facts on File Inc.: 1988

Careers in Education, by Roy A. Edelfelt, VGM Career Horizons: 1988

Careers in Graphic Arts, by Virginia L. Roberson, Rosen Publishing Corp.: 1988

College Placement Annual, by the College Placement Council: revised annually (available in most campus placement offices)

Directory of Department Stores and Mail Order Firms, by the editors of Chain Store Guide, Lebhar Friedman Inc.: revised periodically

Encyclopedia of Careers and Vocational Guidance, Vol. II; Selecting a Career, J. G. Ferguson Publishing Company: 1984

Jobs! Where They Are . . . What They Are . . . What They Pay, by Robert O. Snelling and Anne M. Snelling, Simon and Schuster, Inc.: 1985

National Directory of Addresses and Telephone Numbers, Concord Reference Books: revised annually

Occupational Outlook Handbook, U.S. Department of Labor, Bureau of Statistics: updated annually

The School of Visual Arts Guide to Careers, by Dee Ito, School of Visual Arts Press: 1987

What Color Is Your Parachute? A Practical Manual for Job Hunters and Career Changers, by Richard N. Bolles, Ten Speed Press: revised periodically

INDEX